CW01560631

"…a masterpiece skillfully navigating the maze of a globalized work culture and chronicling in lay terms the mega, beyond state-of-the-art architectural and planning miracle of the Arabian Peninsula."

Liliane C. Koziel, Ph.D., *Peace and Conflict Studies, University of California, Berkeley*

Staying Afloat

Three Years in Abu Dhabi

Steve Burton

iUniverse, Inc.
Bloomington

Staying Afloat
Three Years in Abu Dhabi

iUniverse books may be ordered through booksellers or by contacting:

iUniverse
1663 Liberty Drive
Bloomington, IN 47403
www.iuniverse.com
1-800-Authors (1-800-288-4677)

Photography by Pamela Burton

ISBN: 978-1-4759-3651-3 (sc)
ISBN: 978-1-4759-3650-6 (hc)
ISBN: 978-1-4759-3649-0 (e)

Library of Congress Control Number: 2012915022

Printed in the United States of America

iUniverse rev. date: 09/17/2012

As-salaam alaikum—Peace be upon you

Alaikum as-salaam—And upon you be peace

Contents

Preface

He appeared regal in his starched white *kandoura* and designer sunglasses. Or was it arrogant? Slowly sizing me up, he pronounced, "So *you're* the American hired to build our marinas."

"Yes, sir ... uh, Your Highness."

"There's one thing I want you to remember: the word *no* is not in my vocabulary, and I expect it to be removed from yours."

I was unsure of how to respond to a senior member of Abu Dhabi's Ruling Family. It was the most inspiring, yet daunting, statement I had heard since first setting foot in the United Arab Emirates. Ostensibly, it meant, *You perform to the highest level on the planet and don't sweat the small stuff ... like money.* That is The Rule. The Royal made it crystal clear. It is the mind-set that makes this place a visionary's and master planner's dream, an architect's and engineer's paradise, an inventor's challenge of a lifetime, and likely a business plan nightmare. These folks are redefining the pinnacle of innovation and technology.

A week following the brief introduction to the Royal, I remarked to the CEO of the flagship development company, my new employer, "Abu Dhabi is a mecca of yacht-purchasing power. Why haven't I seen any yacht brokerages in light of the emirate's staggering wealth and incredible growth?"

"It's only Monday," he replied with ho-hum assurance.

Better judgment told me that businesses do not evolve that spontaneously regardless of the prevailing optimistic belief: *If you build it, someone will buy it.* Was the CEO's leap of faith possible? My Western business training was soon to be shredded.

Six months prior to my arrival in the emirate of Abu Dhabi, Yas Island, which is adjacent to the island on which the city of Abu Dhabi lies, was an expansive sandbar. My assignment was to help transform this relatively untouched bird sanctuary into a complex global entertainment and premier yachting destination within thirty months, beginning in February 2007. Included in the overall master plan was a long list of never-before-attempted construction projects that, from my Western perspective, were unachievable within the designated time frame. Six years? Possibly. Two and a half years? No way. To build from scratch a one-off hotbed of extraordinary pizzazz the size of Walt Disney World and Epcot in Florida was the ultimate challenge. I questioned whether, if The Rule were broken, a construction project director would be dropped off in the Empty Quarter, the United Arab Emirates' sandy version of Siberia.

At the time of this writing, the global economy had recently undergone an about-face, aptly described as a meltdown—a debt crisis. Abu Dhabi was not excluded; the crunch was merely postponed. The stories related in this book preceded the economic chaos. The venture was a surreal journey into exclamation points. Boundaries were undefined. How do you prepare for it? Can you? An open mind plus a keen sense of humor proved to be a winning and inspiring formula to assimilate culturally and professionally in this exotic land.

CIA Library—Copyrighted map used with permission

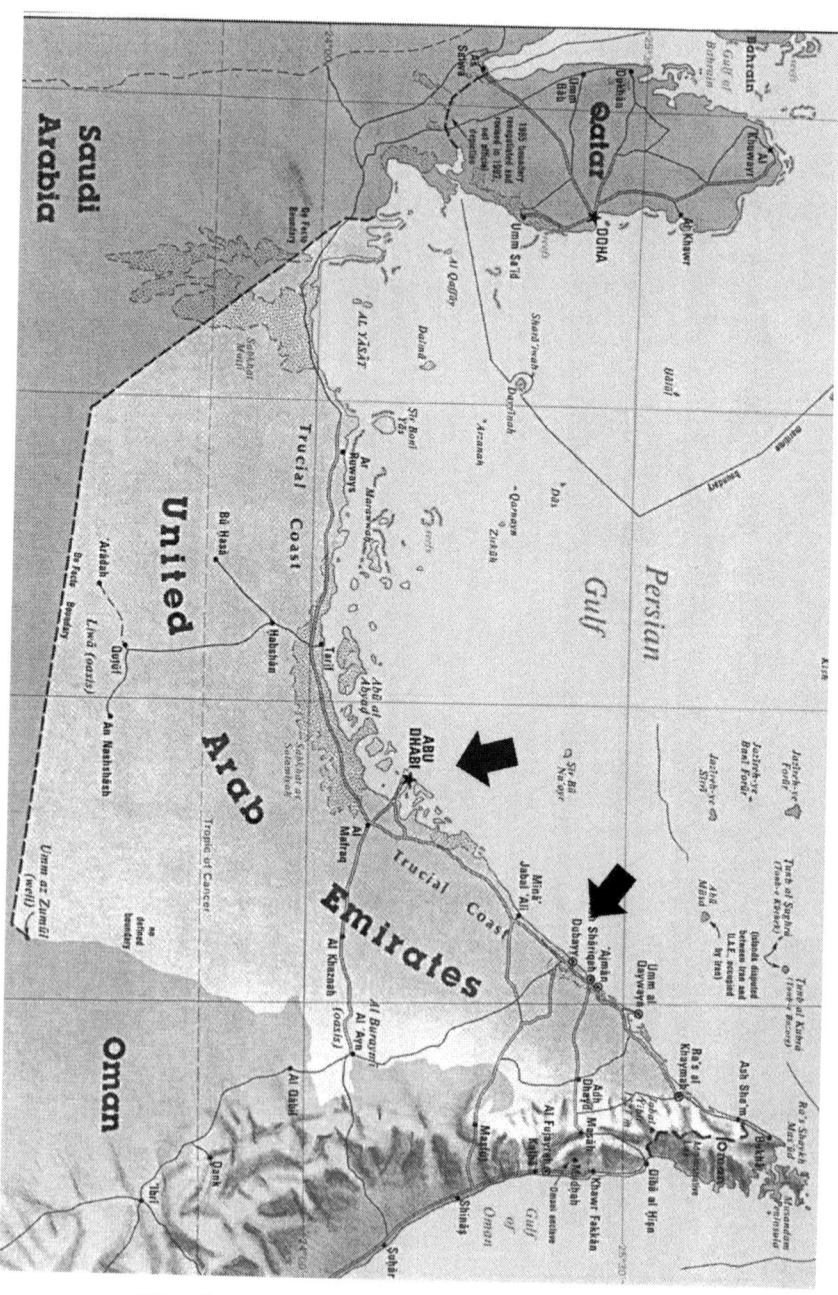

CIA Library—Copyrighted map used with permission

Acknowledgments

Praise to my wife, Pamela, for her willingness to share personal experiences with candor; to Robert and Christine Blackmon, Tom Knight, Donna Galassi, Janine Rush, Julia Roth, Linda Carlson-Freed, Dianne Cloyd, and the iUniverse staff for their support and guidance in keeping my pen headed in the proper direction; and to Fred Carr and Todd Jeffery, my treasured California maritime colleagues who followed me to Abu Dhabi. Take a bow. *Shrukran.*

Part One

The Right Place at the Right Time

Prelude

The global economy was in the fast lane from late 2005 through mid-2008, immediately prior to the bankruptcy declaration by Lehman Brothers, the largest bankruptcy filing in US history. The economy in Abu Dhabi and Dubai redefined *robust*. Money from oil-thirsty countries was propelling this land from third-world to future-world status without a stopover in between. Visionaries and highly skilled individuals were in demand. My wife, Pamela, and I believed we were both. It was early 2007, presumably an opportune time to visit the country and observe firsthand what the media hype was all about.

We both held stable and initially challenging jobs in Northern California, but they had begun to lose their glamour. We'd been accused of being a go-for-it couple, and we were impatient to see what further chapters lay unread. Apprehension had never been much of a roadblock. The halfway point in our lives had been well exceeded, as documented in medical journals and mailers soliciting cemetery plots. As best friends, we had taught ourselves to view as many of life's experiences as possible with an air of lightness, particularly during moments requiring patience to retain sanity. We would soon relearn the value of that virtue—in a big way.

Moving to a sandbox in a Middle Eastern desert was not in the top one hundred on my want-to-do list. Make that the top two hundred. My soles had accumulated a fair number of travel miles during twenty years of marriage, but never had I envisioned that we would pick up and move halfway around the globe, from California to Abu Dhabi in the United Arab Emirates. And *certainly* I had never imagined that I would soon become an integral player on a team tasked by the highest level in the government to undertake one of the most ambitious construction projects in the twenty-first century, which included a luxury yacht marina—in the desert.

What seemed to be an impulsive decision to relocate to the Middle East was, in fact, just that. The decision was not made without careful analysis, facilitated by a notebook of lined paper and a pencil. The line items consisted of an abbreviated list of our life's immediate priorities followed by brief justifications. This approach made it difficult to elaborate on pesky details that might spoil the party—quite scientific. Listening to our souls and following our intuition, the pencil moved with surprising ease. At that moment, we could not envision the extraordinary rewards that an odyssey to this land of superlatives would offer. Picture a child's first step into Toys "Я" Us.

My background includes twenty years in the real estate development and construction industries in Northern California, followed by eight years in the maritime industry, my passion, in the San Francisco Bay Area—dissimilar careers.

My wife's background is equally diverse. Following a career as a real estate broker for fifteen years in Northern California, she pursued *her* passion and began her current career as a freelance photojournalist in the equestrian world. She was invited to cover both national and international horse racing events beginning in 1997. Her comprehensive coverage proved to be a fast-track route to international recognition, and many of those invitations were to the United Arab Emirates. Horse racing and breeding are passions of the Emiratis, and Arabian horses are their heritage.

After making a dozen solo trips to Abu Dhabi and Dubai over ten years, Pamela succeeded in making a convincing case that I should ignore my list of the top one hundred places I'd prefer to see and accompany her on the next trip. I acquiesced—a sign of an exemplary husband. The one-week venture would quickly make my list obsolete.

In preparation for the trip, I Googled several notable real estate development projects in Dubai and researched the greater Middle Eastern territory in *Cliff Notes* style. Dubai appeared to be the celebrity, with its palm-tree- and world-continent-shaped islands; the world's tallest building under construction, soon to reach 830 meters (2,720 feet, or a half mile) high; the world's only seven-star hotel; and a long list of other awe-inspiring visual statements prefaced by "the world's." The United Arab Emirates, also called the Emirates or UAE, and in which Dubai is located, is situated on the Arabian Peninsula and surrounded by larger neighbors—Oman on the south, Saudi Arabia on the west, Qatar on the north, and Iran to the north and east across the Arabian Gulf. Iranians call it the Persian Gulf because they are Persians, not Arabs.

Although I am a relatively open-minded native of Berkeley, California, who was educated at the University of California and whose political convictions earn a wide array of labels, I questioned with tongue in cheek which DuPont Kevlar vest model I should purchase to wear in that volatile area of the world. I presumed that an American may not be particularly welcome. Pamela looked at me like I was anything but college educated.

"Have you ever seen me pack a Kevlar vest in the past twelve years?" she asked.

"Noooo," I replied, struggling to keep a straight face.

"Ignore the tweaked, sensationalistic reporting."

I had prided myself in being able to read between the lines of press reports. Heck, I am *married* to a journalist. Pretending to tuck a tail between my legs, I jumped back into the research. No vest, I figured, would eliminate needless shopping time that could be better spent in a boat showroom. My story begins.

Author and his wife

Dateline: California, April 2007

Passengers with window seats were treated to a spectacular light show as the jet glided into Dubai International Airport at 0100. Strobe lights mounted on the tops of hundreds of towering construction cranes lit up the evening sky. It has been rumored that Dubai is home to 20 percent of the world's construction cranes, and the blinking lights appeared to confirm that rumor. We landed in this land of enchantment in April 2007, following seventeen air hours that ushered us across 8,838 miles—San Francisco to Amsterdam to Dubai. I vividly recall entering the terminal and walking into the biggest jumble of cultures, languages, religions, dress styles, and general chaos that I had ever witnessed. The United Arab Emirates is home to expatriates, or "expats," from an estimated 103 of the world's 196 countries, and it was obvious in the terminal. I visualized a United Nations convention hall at recess. The flight boards displayed connections to every major city on the globe. As an American, I sensed an aura of warmth and collective acceptance among all ethnic groups in spite of the pandemonium. What a far cry from the perceptible racial inequality I recalled as a child in parts of the United States prior to the "I Have a Dream" speech delivered by Martin Luther King Jr. in 1963.

Pamela's Dubai hosts provided a chauffeured drive from the airport to a four-star hotel. Although worn out from sitting in economy class for the better part of a day, my exhaustion was replaced by sheer fear. The kamikaze driver broke most every rule in the California Department of Motor Vehicles' paperback handout. I mentally ran through the fine print of our life and medical insurance policies while observing that the operators of almost *every* vehicle were apparently former race-car drivers. I had never before passed another vehicle at 160 kilometers per hour (96 miles per hour) on the left shoulder. There were obviously unique rules of engagement. Nevertheless, we made it to the hotel, and it quickly became clear why Pamela had displayed annoyance in past travels when I had opted for a lesser-star hotel, like a two.

I rented a car and began to familiarize myself with Dubai during the week that my wife was covering the annual President's Cup endurance race somewhere out in the vast desert sand dunes between Dubai and Abu Dhabi. I visited many of the architectural and engineering marvels that I had researched prior to departing the States. I was intrigued—strike that—*blown away* by the scale and scope of the development projects. *Is this for real?* I wondered. I slapped my face to double-check that I was seeing what I thought I was seeing. *It is for real.* Never before had I seen such frenetic growth in one place.

Dubai was a construction zone on steroids; a beehive of activity; an endless convoy of thousands of twenty-two-wheeled trucks, called lorries, heading in every which direction; a forest of tower cranes; and heavy equipment, scaffolding, and literally hundreds of thousands of laborers. Gigantic dredging equipment, ships, and laborers worked off the coast, reclaiming sand to form immense, man-made islands. Tanker trucks hauling potable water, wastewater, gasoline, and diesel fuel crisscrossed the land. A flotilla of supply lorries carried concrete, steel, rock, glass, marble, transformers, and air conditioners to thousands of construction sites, and packed containers were being unloaded from container ships as fast as port machinery would allow. Roadways, freeways, overpasses, tunnels, waterways, and deep excavations for high-rise buildings and underground infrastructure created a maze of detours, while hotels, restaurants, palaces, mosques, private villas, enormous shopping malls, and world-class sports and entertainment facilities were sprouting like springtime weeds in California. A cloud of construction dust hung over the expanding city. Exclusive of Fridays, the Muslim holy day, disorder reigned.

Viewing what were promoted as the biggest, highest, most ostentatious, and farthest-outside-the-box architectural and engineering projects on the planet, beginning at the Dubai International Airport, exceeded my wildest expectations. Buildings with unique geometric shapes—round, obelisk, sail-shaped—and cloaked in gold, silver, green, blue, and magenta reflective glass looked like ornaments on a Christmas tree. I was apprehensive to venture a guess at the money required to pull off this pageant. The LED screen on most pocket calculators is not wide enough to display the number of zeros.

Mental fatigue set in near the end of that first day of jet lag from viewing what could easily have been labeled "March of Chaos." The shutter on my Canon begged for a shot of 3-in-One oil. Pamela thought I was a babbling fool when we reunited for dinner, especially after I told her that the country's national bird was the construction crane. I calculated that I had another two long days of touring to take in more of Dubai's offerings. Heck, I had not yet hit the Black Diamond slope at Ski Dubai, which cantilevers over the momentous Mall of the Emirates.

Ski Dubai—ah, an amazing piece of pizzazz. It is the last thing I had ever expected to see in a desert. The indoor ski slope, open year-round and temperature controlled at −1°C (28°F), was another of Sheikh Mohammed's creations intended to expand Dubai's diversity. The four-hundred-meter (quarter mile) slope with a sixty-meter (two-hundred-foot) vertical drop includes a quarter pipe for snowboarders. The forty-two-dollar lift ticket, good for four hours of skiing, provides a unique shopping break for a family or ski bum. (The cost of a lift ticket escalated to $58.08 in 2012.) Complete ski apparel and skis and a snowboard are included in the price of a lift ticket, but ski instruction is extra. A quad chairlift whisks skiers to the top of a slope that doglegs out of sight somewhere above Giorgio Armani and Yves Saint Laurent. I viewed the desert ski action through two-story sheets of rigid, clear plastic while seated in front of the gas-fired fireplace at the St. Moritz Cafe.

A dumbfounded American couple seated at an adjacent table shook their heads back and forth while watching two teenagers catch air off a mogul midway down the slope. I could not resist eavesdropping.

"The energy required to power Ski Dubai for a single day is enough to power a midsize Midwestern city for a week!"

I lacked the courage to tell him that, from my biased California perspective, not as much goes on in a Midwestern city that *requires* a lot of power. Besides, did he seriously believe that a resident of Dubai would consider allowing snow conditions to deteriorate from packed powder to slush in order to conserve energy? Get *real*.

Regardless, sore thighs from skiing at Ski Dubai within the lavish Mall of the Emirates in the desert are forgotten as soon as the skier walks outdoors into a 42°C (107°F) furnace. Heart failure becomes the concern.

As a lifelong yachtsman, I was thrilled to see Dubai's white sand beaches and turquoise waters, purportedly home to an abundance of fish and underwater natural wonders. The coastal area appeared opportune for pleasure boating. *I've come this far,* I reasoned, *and Pamela will be tied up with her horse racing gig for another five days. Why not check out the marine industry?* I visited several dated marinas scattered along the Dubai coast and the Creek, a natural-seawater, navigable waterway that extends fourteen kilometers (8.4 miles) inland, dividing Dubai into two parts. The marinas appeared to be fully occupied—a good sign for marina operators but a bad sign for boat sales businesses that depend on a supply of available berths for customers to park new boats. There was evidently an immediate need for additional marinas.

I dropped by the sales office of Nakheel, Dubai's largest (at that time) and government-owned real estate development company. The elaborate models of the company's waterfront projects confirmed that multiple five-star marinas were on the drawing board or under construction. I was intrigued. Another spectator, a Brit named Edward, overheard the many questions I asked the Lebanese salesman. Edward introduced himself as an engineer who was also familiar with the immense projects. As our conversation progressed, he suggested that I visit neighboring, oil-rich Abu Dhabi, the largest of the seven emirates in the UAE, and check out a couple of *its* waterfront development projects. It was, after all, only an hour's drive, and I recalled the astonishing tales of Abu Dhabi that my wife had shared following each return from her prior visits. My new acquaintance called a colleague on my behalf and scheduled a meeting with him the following day in Abu Dhabi. There began a new chapter in my logbook.

Edward's colleague turned out to be a coastal hydraulic and marine engineer from Canada and a project director at the Al Raha Beach waterfront development. He showed me a scale replica of the project, its length spanning half the width of a high school gymnasium. At the touch of a button, miniature high- and low-rise buildings were illuminated. Scale villas, landscaped roadways, a light-rail train system, and meandering man-made waterways dotted with boats provided visual authenticity to the elevated display. The model represented ten kilometers (six miles) of shoreline, master planned to accommodate a future residential population of 120,000 and forecast to be built out in seven to fifteen years. The development was to become one of the largest construction projects in the world. Aha! Four marinas were depicted in the model, all of which appeared to be poorly designed.

My established baseline for fathoming the scope of a project the size represented by the table model was undergoing a sobering ascension. Coupled with Dubai, it appeared that another Roman Empire was in the making. Skeptical that what I was viewing was for real, I asked the engineer who the marina specialists were for this megaproject.

"Specialists? There aren't any," he replied.

"You've got to be kidding!" I exclaimed. "You work for a multibillion-dollar property development company that's building world-class waterfront developments, and there is no one on your team in charge of the basic requirements and needs of a marina?"

"You got it, mate."

Neon signs flashed on the second floor in my skull. I was confident that I knew the marina business from concept design through delivery and operations as well as, if not better than, most in the industry. I sensed that colossal maritime challenges were waiting to be addressed

11

and that the developer, let alone the country, was screaming for expertise. Without hesitation and without regard for where the statement might lead, I volunteered with unwavering self-assurance, "You're looking at someone who knows a lot about marinas."

His expression looked like that of a forty-niner who had just struck gold in an ice-cold California river.

The balance of the day flew by as fast as a bullet train traveling from Paris to Lyon. It included introductions to other project directors—more Brits and a sprinkling of Lebanese, Jordanians, Kiwis, and Aussies, but no Americans—and ultimately to the CEO in the company's downtown corporate office. I was extended an offer of employment four days later, pending the company's receipt and approval of a glut of documentation. I felt like Rocky Balboa jogging at the top of the steps in front of the Lincoln Memorial in Washington, DC, prior to his fight with Apollo Creed.

Following receipt of the employment offer and during the one-hour chauffeured, borderline-sane drive back to the Dusit Hotel in Dubai, I questioned whether the unexpected job offer would be a prudent, let alone realistic, opportunity for me to become an expat for the first time in my life—*our* lives. The company was touted as one of the most ambitious real estate development companies in the world and, evidently, not hurting for liquidity. The job description's challenges were exceedingly high. I would be expected to develop cutting-edge marinas incorporating state-of-the-art technology and assure the highest level of service. The opportunity to work alongside some of the finest talent recruited from the far reaches of the world was unparalleled, and the employment package was attractive. On the flip side, my original intent in accompanying Pamela to Dubai was to be there for support, companionship, personal enlightenment, and pure enjoyment, not to seek a job—honest.

I did not mention the employment offer to Pamela right away. For that matter, I had not completely digested it myself, although I did recognize that it was uncanny how a measure of confidence can overcome uncertainty.

Our return flight to San Francisco was scheduled to depart close to midnight. Prior to packing, I suggested that we celebrate our week's adventures over a glass of champagne in the hotel bar. We toasted, and I asked, "How'd your day go?" faintly aware of the cling of Swarovski crystal.

"Long. But I have enough photos and information from interviews to write some marketable articles. How 'bout your day in Abu Dhabi?"

"It was pretty interesting," I answered nonchalantly.

I shared with Pamela the meeting with the CEO of the development company in Abu Dhabi between sips of champagne. I told her I questioned why I was managing marinas back in Northern California when I could possibly become a part of this magnificent moment in modern civilization. Always the supportive wife, she offered, "All right. Let's check into it."

"I have," I said. "Would you be up for living in Abu Dhabi if I was offered a job?"

"Umm … yeah. That would dovetail into my expanding work in this part of the world," she replied offhandedly, followed by the intuitive question with one raised eyebrow, "Why?"

"I was offered a dream job today—carrying out marina development for the largest development company in Abu Dhabi," I said, flashing an ear-to-ear smile.

"Are you serious? You're serious. Did you accept it? When would you be expected to start?"

"I'm serious. Immediately. I told them I'd first have to discuss the offer with you and, if you were supportive, I'd require at least thirty days after submitting a letter of resignation to my current employer, hold a summit meeting with the family, make preparations to relocate and—"

"Yeah, yeah," she interrupted. "And?"

"The CEO said, 'Okay, I'll see you in thirty-one days.'"

We sat in silence aboard the aircraft for an unknown length of time, contemplating a future of unknowns. Mild intoxication from the champagne back at the hotel bar contributed to the silence. It was somewhere over Turkey that soul-searching elevated to an analytical level. We used a legal pad of lined paper with a line drawn down the center to formulate a blueprint for becoming expatriates. The list was surprisingly short:

Kids (adults)	- Supportive—all four gainfully employed
House	- Rent it
Existing job	- Thirty-day notice of resignation
Cars	- Sell both
Horse	- Leave with sister
Cat	- Just died
Personal belongings	- Ship one-third, store one-third, toss or donate one-third to kids
Friends	- Throw a party
Requested paperwork	- Expedite

"How long do you think we might live there?" Pamela quietly asked the headrest in front of her.

Caught off guard, I shrugged. "I haven't the foggiest." No need to get pragmatic.

Verdict

My mind kicked into high gear, pondering the conversations I'd had with a score of strangers over the past six days. I read and reread the many pages of scribbled notes on the hotel's embossed notepads.

I analyzed and reanalyzed the perceptions absorbed during the entire whirlwind week. Would we readily adapt to a life in this tiny, extraordinarily wealthy, culturally diverse, class-based, monarchical, Muslim country on the opposite side of the globe?

The entire country, including its islands, occupies a total land area of only 32,278 square miles, roughly the size of the state of Maine. In spite of its size, it packs a wallop of global business clout, owing in part to its role in the world's energy markets. One of the project directors at the Al Raha Beach megaproject in Abu Dhabi told me that 10 percent of the entire planet's proven oil reserves lay within the UAE's territorial boundaries—the bulk of it buried in the emirate of Abu Dhabi—and its natural gas reserves rank seventh in the world. Mr. Google confirmed his declaration. The UAE is one of the twelve members of the Organization of Petroleum Exporting Countries (OPEC), and Abu Dhabi, along with neighboring Qatar, has the highest per-capita income in the world. I can live with that.

I could not get my mind off the staggering display of wealth I had just witnessed. I subconsciously fiddled with the leftover dirham currency on the fold-down table on the back of the seat in front of me while deep in thought, ignoring the GPS map displayed on the screen. A palette of eight colors—blue, green, purple, orchid, red, pink, orange, and brown—was incorporated on the notes. Intrigued, I removed a five and a ten US dollar bill from my wallet for comparison and found the familiar green to be the dominant color, accompanied by black on a neutral background. Something didn't compute. Granted, currency such as the British pound, European Union euro, Chinese yuan, Japanese yen, Thai baht, Mexican peso, Indian rupee, Brazilian real, and South African rand each incorporates a rainbow of colors in the minting of their paper currency. But why the Central Bank of the United Arab Emirates did not stick to black on a neutral background was bewildering.

After all, black is the color of its vast reservoirs of crude oil buried under the sand both on- and offshore, waiting to be extracted. Without the development of its oil industry, the UAE of today would likely not look much different than the UAE of forty years ago. The profound significance of the color black was recognized following the first commercially exported shipload of crude oil from Abu Dhabi in 1962, eight years before the country was founded. Today, its abundant reserves are indispensable for the functioning of the global economy as long as oil-thirsty countries remain beholden to fossil fuels. Every day, the world's oil-consuming countries elect to trade a mind-boggling amount of their colorful currency for the liquid gold buried in the UAE's sandbox. Abu Dhabi's cash register is full to the brim. I can also live with that.

But my greatest apprehension was about living in a highly structured, class-based society. Ethnic diversity would be a joy, but the de facto caste system raised a red flag. How would, or could, a native Berkeleyan deal with racial inequality? No one challenges the UAE's hierarchical status quo because doing so would be construed as critical of the monarchical leadership. Expats are guests in their country by choice and are expected to abide by the country's rituals, like it or not. If I were to become proactive in suggesting a change, like marching in front of a palace carrying a bullhorn and placard that advocated equality, I would more than likely subject myself to prison, deportation, or both. I rationalized that the perks from the high standard of living had to, to some degree, trickle down to the labor class and thereby elevate the playing field of servitude. In spite of that hope, it would be a trying doctrinaire hurdle to clear. I postponed further scrutiny in order to ponder as many other issues as possible prior to our arrival in San Francisco—a cop-out.

The passengers seated next to windows had begun to raise the sliding shade covers as the sun peeked above the European horizon, painting the clouds a vibrant pink. Wrapped in a sterilized flannel blanket, I tried to picture myself wearing a coat and tie in 43°C (109°F) temperatures. Abu Dhabi is located a degree above the Tropic of Cancer. The last word in the latitude's identity was disturbing. During the "warm" months of May through September, the prevailing breeze, if any, originates from deep within the blazing-hot desert. Maybe that engineer at the lunch table back in Abu Dhabi was not kidding when he said the only differences between 40°C (104°F) and 43°C are the amount of water consumed and deodorant applied and the consistency of the blood. Goose bumps are a rare phenomenon. *Furnace* is a mysterious word. Clotheslines are used in place of dryers. Glasses fog up and lungs receive a jolt when exiting an air-conditioned building into 43°C. Seasoned residents readily acclimate to the heat thanks in part to climate-controlled buildings. They find the temperature to be delightful when the summer evenings cool down to 33°C (91°F). I envisioned electrical meters spinning at Mach One.

I had also been told that Abu Dhabi—for that matter, the entire country, consisting of seven emirates—was as safe a place to live as Liechtenstein or Andorra. It has one of the lowest recorded crime rates in the world. Since crime is strongly linked to poverty, foreigners are not allowed to extend their stay in the country past the expiration of their visitor's visas if they do not have steady, gainful employment. How novel. Firearms are forbidden, exclusive of law enforcement and military personnel. I recalled a recent CNN news report citing gun ownership in the States at approximately 47 percent of the country's population! The National Rifle Association will certainly not have a satellite office in the UAE. Gangs and their attire are not to be found in the country. Homelessness or hopelessness, tantamount to condemning people to a prison on the streets, is not evident. Graffiti and litter are seldom seen. Emiratis lead a clean and family-based lifestyle. Theft is a dishonor to the extended family—father, mother, brothers, sisters, aunts, uncles, cousins, grandparents, and so on—and is thus extremely rare. Penalties can include lengthy incarceration in a jail tucked away among desert sand dunes under blistering heat. I had zero inclination to check it out.

An Australian master planner, soon to become a close friend, shared an experience from the prior week. He had parked his brand new BMW along a curb on a busy street in congested downtown Abu Dhabi. Because of his unfamiliarity with the pocket key clicker, he accidentally popped the trunk lid instead of locking the doors as he walked away, his back to the car. His wallet, containing 3,400 dirham ($930), and his passport were lying in plain sight on the floor of the otherwise empty trunk. When he returned to his car two hours later, shocked to find its trunk wide open, his wallet and passport were where they had been left, untouched.

He explained that Abu Dhabi's penal code is comprehensive in its endeavor to control unacceptable imported behavior. An expat caught flashing a middle finger in public may face jail time if found guilty in court. I felt relatively assured that I had mellowed since my more reactionary days. The compulsory penalty for an indecent gesture or obscene behavior in public is intimidating. Exclusive of driving, I never—repeat, *never*—observed aggressive behavior during our one-week visit to Abu Dhabi. The Muslim faith disapproves of it, and the country's non-Muslim ethnic groups appeared congenial.

My entire life has been spent living in a democracy—or as close to one as claimed in spite of hard-line influence from uncompromising partisan politicians, avaricious corporations, special-interest groups, and increasing political dysfunction. Abu Dhabi's government operates under the country's framework of a constitutional monarchy. This would be an interesting adjustment. The emirate comprises a president, a crown prince, and many "His Highnesses"

(HH), "His Excellencies" (HE), sheikhs (Sh), and sheikhas, many of whom perform responsibilities comparable to those carried out within the US president's cabinet. Because the Rulers within Abu Dhabi's monarchy all share the same DNA, they are called the Royal Family, or Ruling Family. President Khalifa, one of Sheikh Zayed's eldest sons, was heir to the country's presidency following his father's passing in 2006. The other eighteen sons from Zayed's multiple wives fill both federal and emirate government positions. One of my first purchases following my return to California would be a white board on which to map the extensive family tree, which is a good deal wider than it is high.

The Rulers' names and positions are a mouthful to recite: "His Highness General Sheikh Mohammed bin Zayed Al Nahyan, Crown Prince of Abu Dhabi and Deputy Supreme Commander of the UAE Armed Forces" requires five lines to print in a newspaper column. The column would have to be continued on a later page if he were mentioned twice or the article included another Royal. By comparison, "Barack Obama, President of the United States" requires one and a half lines. And yet, the US president is simply called "Mr. President" or "Obama" by everyone but his wife and daughters. Many expats call His Highness Sheikh Mohammed bin Rashid Al Maktoum, Vice President and Prime Minister of the UAE and Ruler of Dubai, by his nickname, "Sheikh Mo," although it is not uttered in public. Emiratis appear slightly more formal and conservative in both behavior and dialogue than most Americans. But then, who isn't? Maybe Brits.

The economy-class section of an airplane, where people are packed like sardines, is an awkward place to focus on pressing issues. The overweight passenger in the reclined seat ahead of me snored above the drone of the turbofan engines. *Maybe if I faked life-threatening claustrophobia,* I thought, *the flight steward would relocate him to cargo.* The mind strays in bizarre directions, probably a safeguard mechanism designed to bypass insomnia or exhaustion. *Focus. Check the scribbled notes.*

Thoughts clouded my head like pigeons on an Italian piazza. Ahmed, a newfound Emirati friend, clarified my confusion in understanding long Arabic names. Simplified, the first name, without a *Dr., Mr., Miss,* or *Mrs.* preface, is the name most commonly used to address a person—formally or informally, stranger or acquaintance. The second name is the father's first name, and the last name is the family or tribal name. Two-thirds of a name are preordained at birth. Prospective Muslim parents don't have to spend much time dickering over a name choice. However, this is where it can become tricky. A name can be lengthened if the first name of the father's father or the father's grandfather is also included prior to the family name. The extended name further identifies the family lineage. Ahmed bin (son of) Sultan bin Hasan bin Hamdan Al Zaabi is called Ahmed, a difficult name for Western speakers to pronounce correctly. Start with *ah* as in *father*, then force out a little extra air at the end, pause very briefly, and then add *med*. (I respectfully changed Ahmed's four family names.) His father is Sultan, his grandfather was Hasan, his great-grandfather was Hamdan, and they are descendants of the Al Zaabi tribe. His name alone tells me more about his background than I know about many of my closest friends back in California. If Ahmed's sister went by her extended name, she would be Layla bint (daughter of) Sultan bint Hasan bint Hamdan Al Zaabi. Arabic names are easier to decipher than they first appear. Thanks, Ahmed.

A senior director at the company's corporate office boasted that the UAE is essentially a tax-free country, with no personal, federal, corporate, property, general sales, fuel, inheritance, or capital gains taxes. That sounded encouraging. Alcohol is an exception in Abu

Dhabi and Dubai; a 30 percent tax is imposed on legally purchased booze. The populace depends on the government's steady domestic investment even though the government does not receive income from taxation. Fortunately, Abu Dhabi's leaders are benevolent. Wealth has not become a curse. They invest much of the emirate's staggering revenue from its liquid black gold back into their country. The Rulers are on a fast track in their quest to provide the highest standard of living possible for their citizens—best highways and transportation, best education system, best medical facilities, best shopping malls, best cultural attractions, best sports and entertainment facilities and venues, best hotels and restaurants, and so forth. I hoped that air conditioners would be included on the "best" list. Achievement of these goals is a momentous challenge. The Rulers have nonetheless been responsible for their emirate's achieving the fastest transition from third-world to first-world status in modern civilization. Abu Dhabi's living standards have become an inspiration and the envy of the Gulf region. This was particularly noteworthy in that I am a results-oriented kind of guy.

I was amused to discover that Abu Dhabi's nationals take the astounding changes to their homeland for granted, in spite of their very recent evolution from a nomadic Bedouin, or Bedu, society whose main food and livelihood depended on pearls, camels, and dates. Prior to 1960, about the time that Dwight Eisenhower was president of the United States and Harold Macmillan was prime minister of the United Kingdom, no paved roads, medical facilities, schools, or basic infrastructure existed in Abu Dhabi. It was virtually a sandbox, and people lived hand to mouth. Today, Abu Dhabi is a metropolis in the middle of a desert, boasting a Manhattan-style skyline of modern high-rise buildings and many of the unique and iconic architectural and engineering conquests in the world.

Abu Dhabians are proud that their emirate has become a magnet for foreign investment. The United States, United Kingdom, and

21

France have oil interests in Abu Dhabi and maintain a low-profile military presence through high-dollar weaponry sales and training. Western influence and the emirate's pro-Western and pro-Arab leadership promote economic stability, particularly in light of its proximity to Middle Eastern, Asian, and North African countries that are experiencing long overdue political and economic upheaval.

The emirate is now home to one of the largest sovereign wealth funds in the world in terms of total assets, *estimated* at $627 billion in 2012. But then again, it could well exceed $1 trillion. The Islamic tradition of humility and understatement accounts for the Rulers' reluctance to reveal specifics regarding the emirate's investment wealth. Speculating, I figure chances are high that this lack of transparency would be compromised if the government were to try to purchase, say, Greece.

Lost in thought somewhere over the North Atlantic, I presumed the language barrier would be difficult to overcome, although most of the Emiratis to whom I had just been introduced spoke understandable English. Arabic (*a-RAB-ic*) is the official spoken language in the UAE, but English is the business language. English is also the common language spoken outside the office by expats from the developed world. Farsi, Hindi-Urdu, Tagalog, and Russian are widely spoken within their respective large expat communities.

A veiled Arabic secretary back at the company's corporate office told me that the Arabic language would be easy to learn. That was after she uttered, "I speak English very best."

"Pronunciation is strictly phonetic," she continued. "You just need to learn to read from right to left."

Easy for you to say, I mused but did not voice.

She neglected to mention that the Arabic language is considered sacred because it was the language used by God in the revelation of the Qur'an. Because of the language's divine provenance, Arabic words and names may have different meanings and values that a rookie learner must be sensitive not to abuse. Word play—metaphors, figures of speech, and disparaging humor—in cross-cultural communication does not translate well, often to the point of being offensive. Plus, Arabic calligraphy makes Greek look like child's play. The alphabet must first be deciphered before pronunciation homework can begin.

I chose not to bias the kind lady's preconceived opinion of me by sharing an embarrassing moment: Killing time one evening in Dubai, I strolled up and down the aisles of a bookstore and marveled at how books were sectioned according to language. In the area earmarked for Arabic literature, I noticed that books had been placed on the shelves *backward* by a careless employee. The bindings were on the right, not left, side. Concerned about saving the employee from a humiliating reprimand, I flipped the top book on each stack at eye level over to what I thought was its proper position. A stock boy followed behind me a few meters and discreetly returned the books to their original position. Discerning that I eyed his behavior to be rude, he employed his utmost diplomacy in describing to me how to read Arabic, although his brief explanation was spoken in a mix of Urdu and pidgin English, punctuated by hand gestures. I had momentarily forgotten that an Arabic book is read back to front, as well as right to left. I faked a smile and prayed that half of the store's customers were not watching my *faux pas*.

Reflecting on the research I had conducted one evening back at the hotel, I was pleased to read that the UAE's constitution guarantees religious freedom even though Islam is the official religion of the country. *Islam* literally means "submission." Muslims believe they are constantly and continually submitting themselves to the will of God. A mosque, with its towering minarets, is present in every neighborhood. A Christian church can, on rare occasion, be found close to a mosque. Religious conviction is apparently not a concern. Super. I was baptized a Christian, although a church-attendance award has avoided my reach since being anointed while a helpless infant. It was also reassuring to read that disruptive behavior between Shia and Sunni religious sects was not a perceptible issue.

Of utmost importance, how would Pamela and I cope with living in this distant land and leave behind family and friends? *Hey, I reasoned, tens of thousands of expats from all corners of the world and already employed in Abu Dhabi have undoubtedly weighed comparable concerns.* Everyone I had met during the crash-course week appeared to be upbeat and exceedingly thrilled with their relocation. Prolonged second-guessing is not my style. A procrastinator I am not.

The twenty-one hour, relatively sleepless flight back to San Francisco, including a four-hour pit stop in Amsterdam, seemed to pass in record time. A catnap or three helped to shield my brain from overload. Regardless of the pros, cons, and unknowns that evolved from the pragmatic soul search at forty thousand feet, it was irrefutable that a unique opportunity encompassing both of our passions had been offered on a silver platter. Or was it gold? During the wait for our luggage to drop onto the revolving carousel, I made eye contact with Pamela and nodded slowly. "What the heck," I said. "Let's go for it."

She didn't require convincing. Her smile confirmed that she was already onboard. We were soon to become California expats in the Middle East.

* *

I FedExed the one-inch-thick pile of requested paperwork to the company's human resource department in Abu Dhabi within a week.

Notarized documentation certifying my existence on the planet and a copy of the letter of resignation acknowledged by my employer's signature were included. I was also required to send copies of my college degrees along with a certified transcript of my grades, which was no easy chore. My academic records dated back to the days of microfiche, when Bill Gates and the late Steve Jobs were in their young teens. The registrar at the university asked who the hell would want to see *my* grades. A dinosaur bone would be more interesting. I concurred, but proof of a minimum of a four-year college degree was required to qualify for a work visa for a nonmigrant laborer.

Unbeknownst to me at the time, a cursory background security check was protocol. Satisfactory clearance is required before work and residency visas can be issued. I hoped that parking tickets and speeding violations accumulated over the years would not present a hurdle—or the incident back in college when I was pulled over by a campus policeman for pushing a shopping cart with my date seated in it across a street and holding an open gallon of cheap red wine. Heck, any review committee would certainly recognize that as merely one of many initiation rites in the development of a well-rounded, mature, highly skilled dynamo for integration into modern society.

The length of time required to process paperwork in the UAE was baffling, particularly after the company's CEO told me that he expected me to be on the job in thirty-one days. The work and residency visas were not issued until mid-June. It was forty-five days after being offered and accepting the marina development position in April 2007 that I headed back to Abu Dhabi to begin my new job. Pamela remained behind in California to wrap up our move.

A group of American university students seated across from me in the terminal seating area were engaged in lively dialogue while waiting to board the flight from San Francisco to Paris and continuing on to Abu Dhabi. One of the more vocal students, sprawled on the carpet and propped up by her backpack, quoted a recent study to her colleagues that concluded (to my recollection), "Only 37 percent of Americans have a passport. That means that two-thirds can't fly to Canada."

"There are valid reasons," another girl insightfully explained. "Many Americans are uncomfortable with cultural traits other than those with which they are familiar. The cost is high to travel across thousands of miles of ocean to almost anywhere truly foreign. And, the United States is an immense country that offers cultural and geographical diversity within its borders."

I figured she had to be an anthropology major or a travel agent. Continuing, she shared a hypothetical survey item that could have been part of a study conducted by the United Nations and the conjured answers. "Please give your honest opinion regarding solutions to the food shortage in the rest of the world."

I had heard the question and annotations before but was interested in hearing the students' reactions because many of my friends, and probably theirs, are *from* these parts of the world.

In South America, they didn't know what *please* meant.

In India, they didn't know what *honest* meant.

In Europe, they didn't know what *shortage* meant.

In China, they didn't know what *opinion* meant.

In Africa, they didn't know what *food* meant.

In the Middle East, they didn't know what *solutions* meant.

In the United States, they didn't know what *rest of the world* meant.

The students howled. Less-boisterous chuckles were heard from other eavesdroppers. The students would soon discover that the satirical and derogatory profile of different parts of the world carries an element of truth. Was it consolation knowing that these students belonged within the thirty-seventh percentile of US passport holders?

Because my enjoyment derived from mingling with adventurous strangers was evidently apparent, four college-aged, English-speaking Eastern Europeans who had overheard the earlier conversation back at the San Francisco airport corralled me thirteen hours later at Charles De Gaulle Airport in Paris while waiting to board the continuing flight to Abu Dhabi. One of the academic types, wearing wire-rim glasses, asked whether I think it is an accurate perception that a significant percentage of American citizens fall under the stereotype of being either ill-informed or not at all concerned about global issues. He stated that 73 percent of American middle-school children cannot locate Germany on a global map. *How did I happen to end up on an airplane full of inquisitive statistics majors?* I admitted that it *is* a travesty, although I privately questioned the accuracy of his number and did not care to pursue the subject. A couple of my friends in California were schoolteachers and had shared stories concerning many of their upper-grade students' inability to correctly spell words like *geography*, let alone comprehend their meaning in spite of residing in a highly developed nation. I was aware that many young and old alike instead search for the meaning of a word or location of a country on their smartphones and quickly move on. The "Now boarding" announcement got me off the hot seat. I had begun to wonder whether non-Americans construed Americans as being intellectual isolationists. Was *I* being profiled?

A month following my arrival in Abu Dhabi, an Emirati businessman who came across as highbrowed asked, "Does the American interpretation of democracy include and accept subjective news reporting?"

From my point of view, it was a straightforward question with an unambiguous answer—yes. Freedom of the press is a treasured, inalienable right in the United States, and the Founding Fathers never stipulated that the press had to be objective. Rather than dive into a tempting dissertation on the American concept of freedom of press, I listened intently to his thesis on the subject to better grasp his logic. The word *democracy* does carry different connotations in various Arabic countries. He stated that he watched daily world news broadcasts on the BBC, Al Jazeera, Reuters, CNN Europe, and Fox television channels. Persisting, he said, "Why does Fox often have a different take on global political events than the other news agencies, whose reports are generally similar? Is its commentary intentionally biased and more sensationalistic to more effectively attract viewers?"

I empathized with his puzzlement. I have also been known to surf the news channels, but not five of them. My reply advocated that each geographical region or continent, each with its sovereign news agency, may harbor a different perspective than another for innumerable reasons—politics, economy, religion, human rights, or oil. Translated, the agencies' perspectives are based on economic survival and corporate profit, in either order.

Fox has a sizeable viewership in a first-world country. It turned out that the "highbrowed" Emirati businessman had never traveled outside of the Middle East. I wanted to tell those students back at the San Francisco airport that I had stumbled across an adult in the UAE who probably had not accumulated as many travel miles as an average non-passport-holding American, even though his tiny country is surrounded by nine countries within a radius of 800 kilometers (approximately 500 miles).

The businessman was correct on one point: sensationalism does increase viewership. As expats, we would soon experience firsthand how international media can, subtly or vividly, reveal its destructive powers in subjective reporting techniques. The effect on less open-minded readers or viewers can, in a heartbeat, undermine years of constructive dialogue and built-up understanding between ethnic and religious groups. Intentionally or inadvertently, subjective reporting can raise a dust cloud that need not be raised in order to further one interest over another. The annoying aspect is that many readers of subjective reporting may not be as skilled in weeding out issues that create friction or hinder peaceful interaction among otherwise peace-loving peoples. The Middle East is a made-to-order playing field for questionable media influence. We would soon discover that expats, for the greater part, are generally immune to insensitive reporting.

Part Two

---◆◆◆---

Very Bare Essential History

United Arab Emirates
Good stuff to know.

Dating back some two thousand years and up through the 1950s, pearl diving, or "pearling," in the Gulf's pearl-rich waters was the lifeblood for the coastal tribes in the area. They traded pearls with countries as far away as India and those in northern Africa for basic necessities such as food and clothing. At that time in history, the land produced little of economic value, and life was simple, almost primitive. The terrain in what is known today as the United Arab Emirates is generally flat, with barren coastal plains merging into rolling sand dunes of enormous desert wasteland and into fertile areas with mountains abutting the southeastern border with Oman.

In 1968, Britain announced its intention to withdraw from all territories east of Suez after 170 years of controlling force. Without the umbrella of protection, the door was opened for aggressive, neighboring territories to take over the independent sheikhdoms, or Trucial States, that had been established on the Arabian Peninsula. Sheikh Zayed bin Sultan Al Nahyan, the leader of the sheikhdom of Abu Dhabi, recognized the imminent danger and assumed the challenging task of unifying the tribally structured sheikhdoms. A federation ultimately composed of seven sheikhdoms called the United Arab Emirates (UAE) was formed in 1971 under his leadership.

Sheikh Zayed, the undisputed founder of the country, died in 2006. He continues to be revered today as a visionary and statesman extraordinaire, both nationally and internationally. Sheikh Zayed is buried in Abu Dhabi in a courtyard adjacent to the majestic Grand Mosque, one of the largest mosques in the world, capable of accommodating over forty thousand worshippers. The carpet in the main prayer hall, of particular interest to me because of my expanded appreciation of handmade wool and silk carpets, is considered to be the world's largest Iranian carpet. It measures 5,627 square meters (60,570 square feet), weighs 35 tons, and has 2,268,000 knots.

Today, the Emirati people embody a combination of past traditions and cultural practices and modern values. They have a tolerant and forgiving attitude toward the international community, and most understand and accept alternative styles of living and thinking without desiring to alter their own perspectives.

Emirate of Abu Dhabi

Abu Dhabi, meaning "father of gazelle" in Arabic, is one of the country's seven emirates, or monarchies. Up the northern coast lie the other six: Dubai, Sharjah, Ajman, Umm Al Qaiwain, Ras Al Khaimah, and Fujairah. Abu Dhabi is the largest emirate, composing 88 percent of the young country's land area. It is also the wealthiest. It sits on 95 percent of the entire country's proven crude oil reserves, a number that represents 92.9 billion barrels of crude, not to mention 212 trillion cubic feet of natural gas. The oil reserves present in 2012 are forecast to last another ninety-nine years at the current rate of extraction of approximately 2.6 million barrels of crude per day, or 109 million gallons *per day*. The international corporate petroleum giants are thrilled, as are the drivers of vehicles in the emirate, who pay $1.68 per imperial gallon ($1.40 per US gallon in 2008) for government-subsidized petrol.

The *city* of Abu Dhabi within the *emirate* of Abu Dhabi occupies an island that is roughly half the size of San Francisco and separated from the mainland by a narrow, navigable waterway. The island's population is approximately 800,000, comparable to that of San Francisco on a business day. The city is the capital of the UAE and seat of the federal government, analogous to Washington, DC—Dubai being more like Las Vegas. It is often stated within the country: "Dubai has the splash. Abu Dhabi has the cash." I would amend that with, "Abu Dhabi also has splash and an extraordinary amount of cash."

Dubai, meaning "baby locusts," not "leveraged investors," is the largest city in the country and has a story of survival. Its economy has ostensibly been fabricated, and nearly bankrupted, by one of the most gifted and effective marketeers to walk the earth—Sheikh Mohammed bin Rashid Al Maktoum, Vice President of the UAE and Ruler of Dubai. He has created an empire structured around trade, tourism, retail sales, iconicity, and pizzazz to more than supplement the emirate's limited oil reserves. Money from many countries flowed into Dubai's real estate market from 2005 to 2008 as real estate flippers were ecstatically riding their magic carpets. But the genie disappeared in 2009, the carpets lost their magic and were grounded, and Dubai's announced $100 billion debt became intolerable in the waning global economy. Real estate valuations began to plummet.

Abu Dhabi's energy sector's 2009 GDP was $75 billion, or $205 million per day, and yet approximately half of the emirate's entire GDP originates from sources *other* than its energy sector. Economic diversification is at the heart of the government's long-term visionary plan, as it aspires to avoid the pitfalls suffered by neighboring Dubai. "Plan Abu Dhabi 2030," a decades-long plan to replace oil revenue with industry and tourism as drivers of growth, was instituted in September 2007. Energy-intensive industries (metallurgy and plastics), areas where Abu Dhabi has a competitive edge, are expanding. Investment in the aviation, defense, aerospace, and knowledge-based (IT and telecom) sectors are driving its foreign trade. Investment in health, education, and Masdar, a zero-carbon "green city," are contributing to the development of local talent. The emirate is rapidly becoming a global hub for culture, tourism, and leisure. Satellite branches of the Guggenheim Museum, conceptualized by Frank Gehry, and La Louvre Abu Dhabi, designed by Jean Nouvel, are set to begin construction. Dazzling sports and entertainment facilities provide culture and enjoyment for international visitors. Many five-star resort hotels (Emirates Palace and Shangri-La, to name only two) and luxury yacht marinas have transformed Abu Dhabi into an up-market holiday destination. All of these areas require high levels of investment—not an obstacle for Abu Dhabi. It is rumored that even if the emirate's oil revenues were to cease today, its government's diversified investments to date are sufficient to ensure that no Emirati would ever need to work—as in *never*.

Part Three

Dateline: Abu Dhabi, June 2007

By this time, I believed I was as open-minded as a mortal can possibly be prior to becoming a resident of Abu Dhabi. My intention, whether possible or not, was to strive to avoid interpreting and ranking forthcoming experiences within Western parameters. Instead, I was mentally prepared to adjust to a new culture, understanding that I would inevitably stumble over cross-cultural speed bumps in doing so. I was determined to avoid conflict with cynics or jaded expats. Cultural hurdles would not be belittled or judged acrimoniously. I recognized that some degree of a honeymoon period would arise but believed I was prepared. This odyssey would be fun.

Touchdown or Fumble
International flight arrivals to, and departures from, the UAE are typically scheduled for the early hours of the morning. This is not designed to intentionally antagonize passengers but to cater to the airlines' preference to land and take off on a runway shorter than fifty kilometers (thirty miles). As explained, an airplane's wings better meet design criteria after the daytime desert temperatures drop because air molecules become denser and lift becomes greater … *insha'Allah*. If God wills.

The twenty-one-hour return journey to Abu Dhabi included seven airline meals, all meticulously wrapped in aluminum foil.

I have never consumed seven meals on the *ground* in twenty-one hours. Thank God, soon to be called Allah, for French wine. I arrived at the Abu Dhabi International Airport at 0045 only to discover that my new employer had not delivered the work visa to the airport's visa office, as had been confirmed prior to departure. I was unable to pass through the passport check counter despite multiple pleas. No one from the company was waiting in the arrival lobby to pick me up. (A company typically assigns a personal relations officer, or PRO, to a new employee to assist in assimilating his or her life into the Brave New World.) Without a cell phone, now to be called a *MO-bile*, I convinced the semi-English-speaking clerk at the visa window to place a call to the contact name that had been forwarded to me prior to departure. There was no answer—no visa.

There began a two-hour wait on a concrete bench watching hundreds of arrivals stream through the passport counters in the immigration hall. The "contact" answered the fifth call at 0330. He apologized and stated that he would arrive at the airport within the hour with the work visa, *insha'Allah*. Another hour on the hard bench. My rear end was numb. The clerk at the visa window alerted me that the work visa had arrived, and an immigration officer stamped my passport, which sanctioned my stride through the final six meters (nineteen feet), denoting official entrance to the United Arab Emirates.

My four unclaimed suitcases, unloaded four hours earlier, had been locked in a secure room adjacent to the luggage carousel, and the key holder was nowhere to be found. I tried not to envision all my personal belongings being misplaced in Abu Dhabi—like the PRO. Another one-hour wait ensued. The sun was rising. It was setting back in California. I was wiped out and prepared to return to my commemorative bench and crash. By the grace of luck, a young Indian attendant, brandishing a smile as wide as his sandals were long, soon appeared with my luggage on a cart. Had I known of the glitches that I would continue to encounter during the next month, I would have adopted the kid on the spot.

Following release from airport incarceration, the company employee, who was *not* a PRO, dropped me off at a Rotana Hotel in downtown Abu Dhabi. A hot shower followed by a six-hour snooze on a king-size mattress was paradise. When I opened my eyes, I noticed a five-centimeter (two-inch) long red arrow tacked to the ceiling in an unobtrusive corner and pointing in a westerly direction. It was obvious that it did not identify a fire exit unless an axe was available to breach the wall. Curious, I asked the front desk clerk what the arrow signified. Judging from his wide-eyed demeanor, the question apparently pegged me as incredibly naive.

"It points to Makkah, the direction the faithful face during prayer."

Thank goodness I had asked a desk clerk and not a future colleague.

Tough It Out

Although my desire was to begin what I was hired to do, priority shifted to conquering the country's obligatory and exasperating, yet amusing, bureaucracy in order to function smoothly in this culture. Call it assimilation.

The engineer colleague who was most instrumental in initiating this odyssey was on leave. It was the weekend. Why is a weekend Friday and Saturday, not Saturday and Sunday? Do I rent a car? Where are the company headquarters and HR offices located? Where is the PRO? Where is work? *Why am I abandoned?* I purchased a mobile phone at a small electronics shop adjacent to the hotel and called the employee who had picked me up at the airport. He vowed to arrange to have me driven to HR the following morning. Introductions would help to place faces with names on the company paperwork that had been sent from California. My level of self-confidence reached a three-day high, eclipsing my exit from the airplane.

A different employee dropped me off at one of the company's many sprawling construction site offices. I was introduced to several team leaders, provided an office, and handed the keys to a Mitsubishi Outlander to borrow. I later discovered that it belonged to the engineer.

Maybe there isn't a PRO.

Possessing an above-average sense of direction, I stumbled through Abu Dhabi's downtown streets in the borrowed vehicle. Maps were worthless. Either Electra, Defense, and Najda Streets were mislabeled or someone was pulling my leg. How could Twenty-Second Street be on the east end of the island and Twenty-Third Street be on the opposite end and perpendicular to Twenty-Second? Where were street addresses? Who the heck was in charge of laying out this city? No one was able to provide logical directions—*except* the concierge, my new buddy at the Rotana. On his day off, he graciously accompanied me as a guide while driving around Abu Dhabi island. He pointed out banks, auto dealers, Carrefour department stores, Spinneys grocery stores, souks, residential areas, the Corniche, the Iranian dhow port, the ice rink, and many magnificent palaces owned by members of the Royal Family. Consumption of alcohol is forbidden by the Muslim religion, although three federation-monitored liquor stores with no identifying signage are located on the island, theoretically for non-Muslims. My guide included side trips to show me the obscure sites. That by itself earned him a well-deserved tip, which he refused to accept—a cultural conformity that I would soon learn.

Department of Higher Complexity

Nowhere was it mentioned in the employee manual that the better part of a month is required to get a newbie expat's life in order. Fortunately, I was on the payroll during this stage, even though limited time was spent familiarizing myself with coworkers and the company's projects. I initiated a clearly defined mission—select a bank and establish an account, purchase an auto, and find a place to live. A simple punch list. Strike one, two, and three. Each stop required company documentation, completed paperwork had to be translated from English into Arabic, or Arabic into English, by an accredited translator, and then both versions had to be submitted.

I started from scratch at the company's HR office. A pleasant English-French-Arabic-speaking Muslim female employee dressed in a black abaya (*a-BY-ya*) and black shaylah (*SHAY-la*) informed me that all company forms are on Oracle. *Great.*

"How do I access Oracle without a company laptop?"

"What? You haven't been issued a laptop?" she asked incredulously.

I closed my eyes. *Chill. You can figure this out. Persevere.* Subtly, so as not to appear annoyed and certainly not to put anybody out, I said to the upbeat employee, "Kindly tell me where my PRO might be hiding."

The congenial HR lady continued, ignoring my question, "Names are always listed alphabetically by first name, not last name. Have you noticed that you've been addressed by your first name by everyone wherever you've been since you first set foot in our country?"

"Now that you mention it," I acknowledged.

"You are Mr. Steve. I am Noor."

"I like it. Less formal."

I smiled, recalling the number of Mr. Mohammeds to whom I had already been introduced. (*Mohammed* is as common an Arabic surname as *John, Giovanni, Johann,* and *Jean* are in European countries.)

Noor requested my mobile number before I left the HR office, which made sense. Maybe the PRO would find me now. Noor explained that that number is my nationally recognized identification, comparable to a Social Security number back in the States. The mobile number is placed on virtually all paper transactions in the country, and all bank activity is acknowledged via a text message on the mobile. I always felt that some banker was sending me a personal message: "Hey, buddy, you just withdrew 2,500 dirham from your savings account and we want you to know that we know. Do you want to know what your balance is? It's …"

Arrival in any country outside the UAE is acknowledged by Etisalat or Du, Abu Dhabi's two telephone service providers. A text message is received on the mobile within minutes of exiting an airplane and generally before retrieving luggage from the carousel: "Etisalat (or Du) wishes you an enjoyable stay in Istanbul. You may continue to use your Etisalat service by first dialing …"

The temptation to spin around and catch sight of the undercover Etisalat agent hiding behind a trash container always crossed my mind. Upon returning to the UAE, another text message would appear: "Etisalat welcomes you back to Abu Dhabi." Heartwarming.

I walked to the bank closest to the Rotana Hotel to open an account. The company's banking parameters were straightforward: *All* employer compensation package payments (monthly salary and reimbursement for vehicle, travel, furnishings, mobile phone, sports club, school enrollment expenses for children, and bonus, if any) are automatically deposited by the company into an employee's bank account. Out of that account each month come prearranged automatic deductions (housing, sports club, and vehicle). Credit card charges are automatically deducted from the bank account at a predetermined high percentage of the accumulated debt, generally 100 percent, at the end of each month. The system simplifies much of the time-consuming task of managing personal finances. Credit cards have an unusually high annual "user" fee, and checks are rarely accepted anywhere because of the bank's one- to two-week turnaround time. A bounced check due to lack of funds in an account is not pretty for the payer. Punishment for defaulting on a debt under Islamic law, called Sharia, is severe. A stiff fine and jail time are standard, not the twenty-five dollar bounced-check fee common in most Western banking institutions. It keeps a debtor honest.

The new accounts manager informed me that I would have to return with documentation from the company verifying my employment and its guarantee that all compensation package payments were to be transferred from the company's bank into my new account. Again, it was pretty straightforward. I returned the following day with the properly executed paperwork—in English. Damn. I had forgotten the Arabic translation requirement. The duplicate Arabic version was completed the following day, and the bank manager was a happy camper. He had performed his duty to pad the asset side of the bank's financial statement. I had an empty bank account that I hoped would soon receive a deposit. My cultural immersion learning curve continued to remain more horizontal than vertical. Nonetheless, strike one was sidestepped.

My next stop was an auto dealership to purchase a new car. Prior research and dialogue with colleagues confirmed my belief that a Toyota SUV holds its value in the harsh desert environment better than many other SUV models. A salesman at the Toyota dealership informed me that I could not purchase a car without a UAE driver's license. My international driver's license was not acceptable. All right, so I drove my borrowed car to Abu Dhabi's version of the States' Department of Motor Vehicles. Many Western expats have labeled it a "Sub-department of the Department of Higher Complexity." After entering, I wondered, *In which queue do I stand, or does it matter?* It appeared to be a free-for-all, a rugby scrum. Signage was in Arabic. *How will I pass the eye test with Arabic letters?* It didn't matter, because

I was instructed to return with my work and residency visas. Proof of medical clearance from a local doctor is required in the UAE before an expat can receive a residency visa because people with HIV/AIDS are apparently not allowed inside the country, let alone on the streets. Employees of the Abu Dhabi Department of Higher Complexity have evidently never been to California. I returned two days later with the requested documents indicating that I was employed, a legal resident, and healthy. The department also now had a record of my blood type in case of bodily injury due to a traffic accident. Judging from the antics demonstrated by the bloodthirsty drivers, it was clearly forward thinking.

Was it too logical for me to ask why the company does not provide a new employee with a complete package describing *all* needed documentation and guidelines? It could have released a release that should have been released concurrently with the bulk of other releases. Could this be a sign of times that lie ahead? *Stay focused.*

Following two days for translation, two for the weekend, and one for an Islamic holiday, I was handed my treasured UAE driver's license. It was another step toward independence.

I returned to the bank to finance the car. As an unexpected bonus, the bank had a professional relationship with an auto insurance company—a two-for-one deal. The loan officer required company documentation. Why, of course. Silly me. And must it be translated into Arabic?

"Wait a minute," I said. "I just handed you the paperwork from my company eight days ago stating it would transfer every dirham I made into my bank account in this bank. What more documentation could you possibly want?"

I knew the answer before I asked. There *was* no logical answer.

Following ten days of paper shuffling, I appeased the bureaucrats at the Department of Higher Complexity. The final documents were signed at the car dealership, and I was handed the keys to a new pearl-white Toyota Prado. Strike two was history. The car salesman instructed me to select a license plate from a long list of available ones.

"What's the big deal?" I asked.

"What's the big *deal?*" He and others around him gasped.

Historically, certain license plate numbers were reserved for specific people. A Ruler and his entire entourage were all allowed to use the same single digit, say 3. The lower the digit, the more important the owner of the vehicle. To some degree, the law of low digits still applies. Today's license plates are allowed a maximum of five digits. Catchy combinations of double- or triple-digit numbers such as 22, 444, and 123, or four-digit numbers like 5555 and 5678 carry prestige. Police-sanctioned license plate auctions are held periodically during the year where buyers, primarily Emiratis, pay plenty for bragging rights. A single-digit number will sell for upward of $13 million. Although I found this to approach madness, it was not insane to a buyer with an ego and license-plate pocket change. There was comfort in knowing that the proceeds went to charity. My license-number choice was five random numbers—and free.

I returned the borrowed Mitsubishi to the construction site office, where security informed me that I needed a security sticker placed on the front windshield of the new Toyota in order to earn the privilege of experiencing the rite of passage that parking within the gated office complex would offer. I intended to run over the damn PRO if he ever showed his face. I parked the car outside the sacred security gate and walked to my office for two days until informed that the official sticker had arrived. The magical ID was adorned with a top secret magnetic access code, my mug shot, and my name—Mr. Steve.

During those Arabic translation delay days, I scoured the town for a place to live … sans a PRO. Thanks to my Rotana concierge buddy, a rental house, called a villa, was located on the waterfront and reserved. Now my *company* required documentation from the property leasing company. Okay, turnabout is fair play. After all, the company pays the annual rental expense upfront. The week it took for HR to execute the required paperwork allowed me extended time to memorize the flaws in the marble flooring back in the lobby of the downtown Rotana—still my home away from home.

Fait accompli! Bank account, driver's license, car, and residence—completed in twenty-seven days! Patience prevailed. I loved that concierge dude.

Next, I purchased appliances, a bed, and basic necessities and had them delivered—all out-of-pocket expenses. The company's furnishing allowance reimbursement did not kick in until the conclusion of the ninety-day probationary period. It could have very conveniently been mentioned in the employee manual that a wad of discretionary cash would be beneficial prior to an employee's receiving the first paycheck. I had advanced many thousands of dollars to this point.

Visits to the Department of Higher Complexity, occasionally and sarcastically referred to as the Department of Redundancy Department, can nudge a new Western expat without a sense of humor over the edge. The unavoidable tuition is nevertheless invaluable in better understanding the fine print defining *patience.*

Many of the lengthy legwork exercises qualify for the "Rule of Five," a third Western expat cliché. Five is the number of phone calls one has to make in order for someone to answer the phone at the other end. Five is the number of times one must schedule an appointment before someone shows up. Five times as much time, or as many stops, are oftentimes required to accomplish an elementary task as compared to the time the same task takes in the States. The inefficient use of time is adverse to the teachings of Western logic, whereas *non*-Western thinkers would likely ask, *What is logic?* Refusal to get uptight was the best preparation for Rule of Five debacles. It is the sixth trip that sends an expat into orbit.

The territory had become semifamiliar. At the time I informed HR that I had completed getting my life in order, I was introduced to a PRO named Thamer. Was *I* thrilled. Shall I show *him* around? Pamela, traveling with the US Equestrian Team in Brazil, called later that day and buoyantly asked how I was enjoying Abu Dhabi.

"The transition has been a cakewalk," I lied.

Home Sweet Home

The demand for housing in Abu Dhabi exceeded supply in 2006–2008. The cost to lease a villa often jumped 10 to 30 percent per month. The authorities in Berkeley's Department of Fair Housing in California apparently hadn't informed Abu Dhabi's monitoring agency that anything exceeding 5 percent per year is illegal. The monitoring agency, however, comprises wealthy nationals who frown on being monitored. Money travels in one direction. One year's advance lease payment was 235,000 dirham, or $64,383, which comes to $5,365 per month, considerably more than I had been paying for decent digs back in California. At that time, an expat's housing expense was often part of an employee's compensation package.

The *smallest* villa I could find to rent was located on the leeward side of Abu Dhabi island in a large, walled-in compound predominantly inhabited by Western expats. (The reference term *Western expat* is henceforth used generically to include any highly skilled individual from a developed country.) "Small" was a 465-square-meter (5,000-square-foot), two-story, five-bedroom, six-bath, marble-floored behemoth with twelve-foot ceilings and separate housekeeper's quarters. It was a gargantuan echo chamber. Window coverings and kitchen appliances were not included, although five of the bathrooms included a bidet, perfect for washing underwear or wringing out a mop. The walled-in backyard with no landscaping was a cat's paradise—a big sandbox. Our furniture, in ocean transit from California to Abu Dhabi via a stopover in South Korea, would not begin to furnish a quarter of the villa. Prior to leaving California, I had no idea how much or which of our belongings to ship because a future residence was an unknown. The company's furniture allowance was apparently designed to partly alleviate the spartan look of the warehouse.

When construction of a house is completed in the States, protocol, as I have always known it, includes a clean-up crew to spruce it up prior to the arrival of residents. It's not so in the UAE. Our Abu Dhabi villa was brand-spanking new, and we were to become its first occupants. The floors, walls, windows, stairs, kitchen, bathrooms, and cabinetry were coated with construction and fine desert-sand dust. Two of the toilet bowls offered exercise pool privileges for several physically fit cockroaches. I informed the leasing company that the clean-up crew had apparently gotten lost on its way to the villa.

"No. That's your responsibility. Just hire a bunch of Indians," the leasing agent replied, rolling his eyes in recognition of my obvious ignorance to life in his country.

The security guard at the entry gate to our villa compound provided the mobile number of Babu, an Indian who operated a cleaning service. The "service," composed of seven sandaled workers, arrived on vintage, single-speed bicycles. One of the laborers had a hose slung over his shoulder like a bandolier, and four others carried long-handled squeegees resembling coat-of-arms flags. A vacuum, broom, rags, and toilet bowl brush to swat cockroaches would, I assumed, certainly follow. I watched in wonderment as the seven exterior doors were opened and the hose hauled upstairs. Seven sets of fluorescent teeth belonging to the dark-skinned, smiling Indians lit up the hallway. That temporarily eased my apprehension until water began to cascade down the marble staircase. In disbelief, I ran upstairs only to gasp as the walls, including electrical switches, windows, countertops, cabinetry, and bathrooms were hosed down as if they were on fire. Sacrificing civility, I waved my arms and let loose with a litany of obscenities. The head hose honcho stated with a reassuring smile, "Do we all time."

"Bull*shit*," I stated in unmistakable, erudite English that eluded the Urdu-speaking boss. He was obviously unaware that I had constructed many houses in earlier days and was familiar with acceptable procedures.

The six squeegee wizards pushed what had become a lake on the marble flooring out the open doorways. Following thirty long minutes of visual torture, the cleaning crew bobbed their heads back and forth with appreciative smiles, indicating the job was completed to their satisfaction. I was prepared to strangle someone. Shall I dare reach for a light switch and chance electrocution? That would not bode well for my wife, who would discover my stiff body lying on the marble floor with hair sticking straight out when she arrived in another week. In the exasperating hour that followed the crew's exit, the water that coated the entire interior of the villa, floor to ceiling, evaporated. Why, of course! All of the doors were open, and it was 41°C (106°F) outside. What a steal! The entire power-wash job cost a mere 100 dirham ($27). Then I grasped "Do we all time."

If newly constructed houses in the warmer climes of the States incorporated marble flooring and many exterior doors, the reduced construction clean-up cost might knock a thousand dollars off the sales price—more if Babu were the boss.

The twenty-foot container, partially filled with personal belongings that we felt were important to ship from California, landed five long weeks after my arrival. Pamela arrived at midnight three days later, not in a container. I picked her up at the airport in the recently purchased Toyota Prado and escorted her to our new home away from home. It was the first time she set eyes on the villa. I had placed the few pieces of furniture, three throw rugs, four towels, and hanging clothes where I hoped they would be acceptable. Sadly, a 220-volt villain had cremated the 110-volt CD player. Her jubilant smile eased my anxiety after she completed a tour of the vast premises and located the air-conditioning thermostats. I handed her the dozen yellow roses that I had hidden in the refrigerator and said, "Welcome home."

A story accompanies the chivalrous deed. As I exited the flower shop the day preceding her long-awaited arrival, I inadvertently bumped into an Arab gentleman, nearly losing my grip on the bouquet. He apologized for his blunder, although I was clearly the one who had failed to yield. We struck up a cordial conversation, and I revealed my reason for purchasing the flowers. He explained that he was from neighboring Saudi Arabia, a fundamentalist Islamic country, and the sale of roses to celebrate Valentine's Day is borderline banned there by the Commission for the Promotion of Virtue and Prevention of Vice, or religious police. I told him that I thought Valentine's Day, which the current day was not, was a day designated for all, regardless of religion, to dedicate quality time to those we love. In Saudi, he continued, a rose exchanged between two lovers is construed to be a small idol that they worship, and the couple deserves punishment for deviating from traditional religious values. It is believed to be a Western cultural invasion that furthers the erosion of morals. I thanked him for the cultural enlightenment and entertained the idea of tossing the bouquet into a refuse container. Fortunately for my wife, I didn't.

The first priority, following the roses, was to obtain Pamela's residency visa. I had previously downloaded a UAE Immigration and Visa Department guide that identified location, work hours, contact details, and services. A paragraph entitled "How to deal with visa and document processing problems" was an example of how some facets of business mechanics and conduct have stalled at a second-world stoplight:

> If you find yourself in a conflict or with a problem at the Immigration Department, the same guidelines apply to dealing with bureaucrats in the UAE as they do anywhere. Don't lose your cool, be polite, and depending on the situation, you have to decide whether to be persistent vs. giving up vs. trying to find someone else to deal with. Wasta can help with awkward situations—many rules in the UAE have a certain element of flexibility—but don't count on it. Go away and try again another day is sometimes a solution to a problem. Attractive, young, blonde-haired women seem to have fewer difficulties and speedier document processing than other people for some inexplicable reason. If you have a friend who fits that description, send her along to do the job for you.

"They've *got* to be kidding," Pamela sneered.

"The directions sound aboveboard to me," I replied. "Take it in stride. You're a blonde."

Blonde or not, attaining the residency visa required forty-five days of trial and tribulation at the Immigration and Visa Department. Granted, she arrived the day before Ramadan began. An influential individual within the Abu Dhabi government whom I had been fortunate to meet listened to our woe and issued a directive that was couriered to some mystical location. Her residency visa was in hand at 1700 that afternoon, thereby bypassing Secretary of State Condoleezza Rice's desk in Washington, DC. Nationals know the shortcuts and have the connections to access scarce resources, called *wasta*. Pamela was in.

Part Four

———◆◆◆———

"Heigh-ho! Heigh-ho! It's off to work we go."
—*Snow White and the Seven Dwarfs*, Disney, 1943

"It may be those critical months or years of turning cultural bewilderment into concrete understanding that may instill not only the ability to think outside the box but also the capacity to realize that the box is more than a simple square, more than its simple form, but also a repository of many creative possibilities."

—William Maddux and Adam Galinsky, 2007

If You've Got It, Flaunt It

The month of red tape had been an enlightening crash course in perseverance. Finally, I was moving onward to full-time work. My responsibilities when hired were to oversee the design, development, delivery, and implementation of the operation of three or four five-star marinas and a boat service center. The word *or* was perplexing. The number of marina projects jumped to six within four weeks, to eleven by the sixth week, and then included the development of a blueprint for a comprehensive water-taxi service to be employed on a yet-to-be-built waterway system weaving through one of the company's immense, yet-to-be-built developments. *Or* apparently meant that today's plan would be outdated tomorrow. I reflected on my question to the CEO prior to being hired: "Where are the yacht sales businesses in Abu Dhabi?" His matter-of-fact reply, "It's only Monday," possibly had merit.

Numbers in the high hundreds of thousands of dollars defined my average spending ceiling on a construction project as a building contractor in California prior to relocating to Abu Dhabi. Project specifications were detailed, jobs were bid, line items were generally awarded to the lowest bidder, and cost controls were paramount. I adhered to capitalistic business procedures learned as far back as junior high school, when my spending allowance was earned by raking leaves and mowing lawns. In Abu Dhabi, the words *hundreds of thousands of dirham* had become passé. The word *thousands* was replaced with *millions, hundreds of millions,* and—ho-hum, *billions,* lots of them. If there was a spending cap, it was an unknown.

In 2007 through 2009, the cost of many of the construction projects on which I worked was implausibly higher than a business financial plan could justify. Investment strategy was not textbook. The global supply of human resource talent was stretched and its demand high. Master planners, consultants, architects, and contractors charged outrageous fees, knowing that their availability, expertise, and promise to perform within sometimes unattainable deadlines were their ace cards. Iconic conceptual structures were launched from drawing boards with lightning speed. Project approvals were made with equal rapidity and without an accountant's review for economic viability. The process of competitive bidding (or *tendering,* in everywhere-but-the-United States speak) on a project often produced numbers that turned out to be more cosmetic than realistic. A plan to service and maintain finished projects was absent. When, or if, a business plan was requested midway through construction, it would more than likely not make financial sense. The red ink disappeared into the ozone. It was a classic case of placing the cart ahead of the horse. The underlying mentality was "actualize the Rulers' visions" and "there is plenty of money in the cash register." It was about this time that *"insha'Allah"* became a germane term in my vocabulary.

The pot of money for projects was apparently bottomless … and nontransparent. Other than the Rulers, no one knew how big the pot was. Western expats and Abu Dhabi's nationals were surrounded by opulence and lived a privileged lifestyle. Some could say they were spoiled. Consumerism was alive and well. A Western expat's attractive compensation package justified an oblivious stroll past a gold-bar-dispensing machine under twenty-two-carat, gold-leaf-covered domed ceilings in the Emirates Palace Hotel on the way to high tea (with one scone, of course) in the tea lounge at $115 per person. My $260 birthday cake at the Shangri-La Resort Hotel was liberally frosted with edible flakes of gold leaf, a gesture that had never been extended back in California. We became lovers of spectacle. Exotic vehicles were, and still are, as prevalent as Chevy vehicles in the States. Wealth was flaunted. Expat colleagues called it "play money." We were lulled into complacency.

Fearless and Innovative

My new colleagues exuded confidence and fearlessness. To them, no task was too formidable. They were ingenious innovators. They thought outside of the box. Many of the company's projects under construction appeared to defy the laws of physics and seemed to be impossible to erect, but practicality was not always a relevant issue. How will a window washer safely access concave surfaces on the exterior of a high-rise building? How can a load of concrete be lifted almost one kilometer (about half a mile) without its setting up in building the Burj (Arabic for "tower") Al Khalifa in Dubai? How will an individual be able to ascend its 160 floors in an elevator through two microclimates in sixty seconds without the onset of a nosebleed? How will an Emirati recoup the cost to build his spiral-shaped building?

Beginning on day one, I was immersed in long numbers and iconic "wow" projects, using superlatives like none I could ever have imagined. They were the focal point of meetings, research, reports, and media. All had one common denominator—deadline. A deadline could not, under any circumstances, be broken—period. Senior project directors operated like conductors of orchestras. The unfathomable number of challenges, each with Olympic-level hurdles, raised the ante to a level likely never before experienced in the twentieth or twenty-first century. The orchestra's sections were composed of architects, designers, consultants, engineers, and builders recruited from all corners of the globe.

Sometime during my first week on the job, a group of brainy colleagues handed me a piece of paper with three rows of three dots, each arranged in the center like a game of tic-tac-toe. I was handed a pencil and instructed to connect all nine dots using only four straight lines without removing the pencil from the paper. I scribbled for ten minutes, working within the immediate perimeter of the square without success. One of the smirking onlookers in the bleacher seats stated with exaggerated exasperation, "Think outside the box, mate."

Of course! After another five minutes of wrestling with lines, I discovered that it *is* possible. Two of the four straight lines must extend well beyond the square of nine dots. A couple of back slaps acknowledged my apparent acceptance into the OTB (Outside-the-Box) fraternity. The initiation rite was a bit more upbeat than the degrading ones associated with the Greek system that I experienced back in college.

Baling Wire and Duct Tape

Several weeks following my hire, I observed that the two-year-old, nine-meter (twenty-eight-foot) Gulfcraft runabout boat that had been assigned to me as critical to marina responsibilities begged for maintenance and TLC. The fiberglass hull below the waterline required a pressure wash to remove two years of accumulated marine growth, followed by a light sanding and application of a coat of primer and bottom paint to discourage future growth. The hull and deck surfaces above the waterline were in dire need of a buff and wax job. The twin 250-horsepower Mercury outboards had no record of ever being serviced, and all canvas coverings were faded and partially ripped from exposure to the sun's intense ultraviolet rays.

My search around the perimeter of Abu Dhabi island for a boat service center equipped to service the company boat was brief. The only game in town that I found capable of a haul-out reminded me of a scene from a movie filmed in Hong Kong that depicted waterfront activity in the 1800s. The boatyard was archaic and chaotic. Unrecognizable boat parts were strewn about haphazardly, and the working conditions were perilous by Western standards. Only Hindi, Urdu, and a touch of Arabic were spoken. It was prayer time when I strolled into the yard, and a dozen laborers knelt on their prayer rugs facing Makkah as the muezzin's melodic call to prayer was broadcast from a neighborhood mosque. Were they seeking divine intervention to avoid an unforeseen "oops" that would more than likely occur to a boat entrusted to them by its owner? With trepidation and after bartering 25 percent off the already-low scribbled quote, a handshake sealed the deal to have the boat thoroughly serviced. I elected to surrender my anxiety and go with the flow. Not a word of English had been spoken. Sign language and a shared understanding of boat maintenance were all that were necessary.

Traditional Emirati boatyard with basic amenities

The next day, I returned to what I had privately nicknamed the Baling Wire and Duct Tape Boatyard to check on the job's progress.

The boat had been removed from its trailer and propped up on four rusty steel drums with tread-bare truck tires used to cushion the hull. How did the boat get up there? I thought it best not to go through the theatrics to ask. The crew of Indian laborers nevertheless demonstrated superb workmanship and offered Cheshire-cat smiles and the traditional head bobble. A power tool was not to be seen.

I piloted the now-pristine company boat on a half-day cruise around Abu Dhabi island to view the pleasure-boating culture. "Underwhelmed" was a descriptive understatement. The eight- to twelve-meter (twenty-six to forty foot), inexpensive, UAE-built fiberglass boats berthed in the seven existing older marinas constituted 75 percent of the 901 total berths. The eleven marinas, soon to become fifteen, in my marina portfolio represented another 2,200 berths. Other waterfront-development companies in Abu Dhabi had concurrent plans for marina projects. Could, or would, this emirate grow from 901 berths to 6,000-plus and become a pleasure-boat mecca within five years? The master planners and Rulers thought so. It represented growth in excess of 90 percent per year. I, however, had *very* serious doubts.

My cruise around the island as a pleasure boater was anything *but* pleasant. One of the evil-looking, high-powered marine police vessels with flashing red lights hailed me to a stop as if I were on the Most Wanted list. Even though the name of the company was emblazoned on both sides of the boat and the boat itself was probably familiar to them, the marine police officers requested that I provide the vessel's registration, an ID card, and my route and destination. After fifteen anxious minutes, I was cleared to continue. Twenty minutes later and ten kilometers (six miles) farther down the waterway, I was again pulled over by a triad of marine officers on a different marine police vessel. When asked for the same documents as before, I asked the senior member of the crew to kindly call the other police vessel back in the direction from which I had just traveled to confirm that the company boat and I had already been checked out and declared legal and were not a threat to the country. It was my misfortune that he did not speak or understand passable English, and I did not speak Arabic. After another fifteen exasperating minutes, I was motioned to head on my way. Now my hackles were up. I was theoretically in a pleasure craft on a pleasure cruise and abiding by navigational laws learned from many years of boating in the States. In the end, my half-day cruise around the island resulted in *four* stops by marine police vessels. I was disheartened, envisioning a navy of marine police vessels plying Abu Dhabi's waterways after new marinas were brought online in the near future. Another challenge was tossed on the surprise pile.

Waterway laws, environmental regulations and provisions, and boater-safety guidelines were essentially nonexistent within the emirate's small boating community. Navigational charts and markers were often undependable due to constant dredging activity. The shape of the shoreline was continually modified to accommodate expanding waterfront development. Sand islands were created or reshaped, and navigation channels were frequently altered. The bureaucracy required to procure an entry or exit visa into or out of the emirate, let alone the country, for both crew and yacht was a labyrinth of red tape. A pleasure-boating culture was clearly in an embryonic stage. I recruited a reputable marine attorney from San Francisco, California, soon after my exploratory boat trip. His mission was to initiate dialogue with the many fragmented government maritime agencies that would ostensibly oversee pleasure boating in Abu Dhabi's waters. The success of his assignment was crucial.

Fred arrived in Abu Dhabi exactly one year after my own arrival. I picked him up at the airport at 0100, and we returned to my villa where he remained as a guest for his first month. I had learned the nuances of being a personal relations officer and figured I could ease his assimilation through the Departments of Higher Complexity. After he freshened up and uncrossed his jet-lagged eyes, I informed him that he would be a keynote speaker at the first gathering of the heads of government maritime agencies.

"When is this meeting to be held?" he asked.

"In six hours—0900."

"Wait a minute. What's the subject? Who will be present? I just arrived! What does this place look like when the sun's up?"

"Relaaax," I said reassuringly. "I'll introduce you and provide the audience a little background. Just pick up on the subject matter and BS your way through. You know how to do that. You're an American attorney. Be courageous. You are going to be the Boy Scout leader for the emirate of Abu Dhabi, and your collective guidelines may be adopted at the federal level."

I had never before seen an attorney stammer. Fred was getting a taste of what I had experienced on *my* first day on the job. By the time he completed his talk, his professional demeanor, ability to engage the audience, and comprehensive maritime knowledge had earned him immediate acceptance and credibility.

Three weeks following Fred's hire, he received a call from a project director who requested that he hustle down to the port and "assist some boat people with a customs problem." Fred anticipated that he would be dealing with a boatload of Iranian refugees. Instead, he found himself on the bridge of one of the world's largest sailing yachts. Her crew and guests were mired in the country's entry visa bureaucracy, so a competent maritime attorney was just what the doctor ordered. Although only three weeks into his new job, Fred thought he had died and gone to paradise, at least until I asked him to figure out how to get the marine police to chill.

The Arabian Gulf's political volatility presents legitimate reasons for the in-your-face national-security precautions in Abu Dhabi. Oil and natural gas are, to a great degree, the lifeblood of the coastal countries and a precious global commodity. Abu Dhabi island is only 220 kilometers (136 miles) from Iran as the crow flies. On a clear day, Iran can be seen with the naked eye across the fifty-kilometer-wide (thirty-mile) Straits of Hormuz from the northern end of the UAE. The strait is the most strategically important choke point in the world. An estimated 15.5 million barrels of crude oil transit the Straits of Hormuz each day. Once inside the Gulf of Arabia, the shipping channel weaves through many large, restricted tracts of water that mark offshore oil and gas fields, and Abu Dhabi owns many of these navigation-restricted tracts. Any destructive action by hostile forces that may have a damaging effect on the emirate's well-being will invite a retaliatory response likely supported by pro-Western, oil-reliant nations. A pleasure craft cannot merely cruise from a marina in Abu Dhabi out into the Gulf on a fishing excursion or cruise to Dubai without first filing a "flight plan" with the Coast Guard (renamed the Critical National Infrastructure Authority, or CNIA, by presidential decree in May 2007) and having knowledge of where to and where not to cruise. National security is paramount.

Looking ahead, my concern was how the diversity of new pleasure boats that would theoretically make up the estimated six thousand vessels envisioned by the Rulers within possibly five years would achieve a compatible existence with the emirate's watertight security apparatus. New berthing availability in wealthy Abu Dhabi would attract vessels significantly larger and more sophisticated than the small, inexpensive boats that currently occupied most of the island's existing 901 berths. Thousands of these vessels would have the capability to travel well offshore, even to neighboring emirates and countries both within and outside the Gulf. Fred had his work with the government cut out for him; he had to retain the word *pleasure* in a recreational boating culture that was in its initial stages and positioned to explode.

Momentous Yas Island Project

Some of mankind's largest single projects—the Great Pyramid in Giza, the Colosseum in Rome, the Parthenon in Athens, the Panama Canal, and the Palm Jumeirah in Dubai—required many years and many thousands of workers to complete. Abu Dhabi's Yas Island project was developing into one of the most ambitious construction projects ever undertaken in the twentieth and twenty-first centuries.

Yas Island is one of the two hundred islands in Abu Dhabi's archipelago of sandbars. It is one-third the size (twenty-five square kilometers, or 9.6 square miles) of Abu Dhabi island. A narrow waterway separates the two islands, and each end of Yas Island is connected to Abu Dhabi via a bridge and a ten-lane highway, all completed in 2009. Dredging modified the size and shape of the original island in 2006 in order to generate fill material required for another waterfront mega-development across the channel on the mainland. The natural habitat of environmentally sensitive, shallow-water-growing mangrove trees that thrive in salt water and partially surround Yas Island was, fortunately, spared during the dredging operation, a surprise in light of the no-nonsense pace set to develop the sandbar.

Abu Dhabi's Rulers made the decision in 2006 to upgrade the master-planned motor sports racetrack on Yas Island into a permanent track designed to Formula One specifications. The final race on the 2009 Formula One, or F1, Grand Prix circuit was soon thereafter scheduled to be held on the island on November 1 of that year. Because the racetrack was designed to encircle part of a marina, the vision was named Yas Marina Circuit: Home of the Formula 1 Etihad Airways Abu Dhabi Grand Prix—quite a mouthful. Once completed, the racetrack would become the most technologically advanced F1 Grand Prix racetrack on the planet. Covered seating for forty-one thousand spectators and lighting for nighttime racing would be included—both firsts. Of the four five-star marina projects on which I had begun working simultaneously, the Yas Marina moved to the top of the priority list.

The entire island project employed forty-five thousand migrant construction workers who worked day and night. The village built to house the laborers and the logistics required to transport them were feats in themselves. Hundreds of buses were dedicated to moving the laborers around the clock to dozens of locations, most of which changed weekly. Workers were provided with food, clothing, medical facilities, barbers, and cricket fields. More than 1.67 million gallons of water were consumed every day on the island. According to *Yas Island: Race to the Finish*, approximately 12,000 fresh loaves of bread; 28,000 pieces of Arabic bread, called *naan*; and 156,000 pieces of Indian bread, called *chapattis*, were prepared daily in the village. And, not to be overlooked, 210 tons of fresh vegetables, 1.7 million eggs, and 1.3 million pieces of fruit were consumed each month. An enormous supply of lamb used in the preparation of many curries, a fond food staple of the Asian ethnic groups, kept the sheepherders hustling. The owners of neighborhood grocery stores were cut out of the food supply chain by virtue of the sheer volume.

It was not uncommon that orchestrated teams working simultaneously on multiple projects stepped on one another's toes. During many phases of construction, their respective projects' plots of land overlapped. It was essential that the parties engage in textbook communication and cooperation. Issues and problems were brought before senior project directors on a daily basis, and solutions and alternatives were discussed and approved within a matter of hours, not days, weeks, or months. All inspections were handled by the core team with the assurance that their combined knowledge and global track records were the best of the best.

I was astounded when I learned that architectural and engineering teams did not have to jump through an extensive list of regulatory hoops prior to their construction plans' receiving a stamp of approval before beginning a project. From my general contracting experience in California, the layers of Western government bureaucracy often required years to clear. But detailed reviews and clearances from environmental, earthquake, and flood control agencies were nonexistent on Yas Island. Approvals from the fire, power, water, sanitation, and waterway departments were often given during construction or after the fact, if at all. There were no unions, no citizen or political action committees, and no attorneys. A vote requiring a two-thirds approval was unnecessary. We were under a deadline. The F1 race was on the international calendar, and the November 2009 project completion date was not negotiable.

Expediency was easy to implement. Because Abu Dhabi is a monarchy, the approval process consists of a Ruler's yea or nay. Once a plan or drawing is presented, a nod is all that is required to either return it to the drawing board or proceed as submitted—immediately. A detailed project cost breakdown is an impediment to progress. If Dubai's colossal construction achievements are a working example, then maybe, just maybe, this Yas Island project could be pulled off in thirty months. I was becoming a believer.

Part Five

Red Flag

Class-Based Society

A caste societal system did not sit well with me when I was initially weighing the decision to relocate to Abu Dhabi. To achieve a comfort level—call it a tolerance level—I had to better understand the history, reasons, ramifications, and rationale that qualified this country's entry into the fraternity of recently emerged nations. Was this system any different than my housing a nanny or an au pair back in the States?

The UAE was under British influence as recently as forty-five years ago. For that matter, a significant part of the entire planet has been under British rule or persuasion to further its commercial interests at one time or another during its five-hundred-year empire. Colonial influence has left its mark on the UAE today: its class-based society is one of the more visible.

Simply and unashamedly stated, the hierarchical order that has advanced the country into the twenty-first century comprises three classes—labor, brains, and bank. There has been no apparent attempt to challenge or modify the status quo. Those of us from countries with a flatter societal structure understood that we were guests in a country that incorporated a system that works for it.

Approximately 84 percent of the country's 5.1 million people are nonnationals, called expatriates or expats, both skilled and unskilled (based on the semireliable 2011 census—emphasis on *semi*). Numbers fluctuate radically as working expats enter and depart the country. The unskilled, semiskilled, and simple-educated expats account for half of the country's population, or 2.5 million people. This lesser-developed labor force is predominantly composed of migratory workers who belong to South and Southeast Asian ethnic groups—Indians, Pakistanis, Bangladeshi, Filipinos, Thais, Sri Lankans, and Nepalese. They choose to work in the UAE on temporary, but renewable, work visas.

Those in the country's migrant labor class work and behave as if they have been raised to be at the beck and call of their employers. Maybe they were. It is possibly their station in life. Many Emiratis demonstrate little respect for them even though the labor class essentially built the country. I, nevertheless, found that these unsung workers take immense pride in their work. It is an embarrassment and insult to them for an employer to take a job away from them. With few exceptions, they are provided room and board, health care, and a round-trip airline ticket to their homelands every year, sometimes every *other* year, for a thirty- or sixty-day reprieve. Their passports are surrendered to their sponsors between visits. They earn a small income, most of which is mailed home to their families in absentia. A housekeeper receives approximately $240 per month, and a construction worker $270 per week, working ten-hour days and six-day weeks. This is more money than they would ever receive for work back in their native countries.

Is it blind justification to rationalize that, with few exceptions, the living and working conditions for the labor class are infinitely better than the quality of life left behind in their homelands? Am I, or anyone outside of the labor class, qualified to define *quality of life*? Each worker sacrifices a presence with his or her family in order to provide what is perceived to be a better standard of living for the extended family back home. Regardless of their reasons, I developed great respect for the service class and always conveyed my sincere appreciation to those who provided the expected service, often to the arrogant consternation of their employers. An elitist or equal-opportunity offender I am not.

Emiratis, or nationals, have established a stratospheric benchmark for expected customer service. Make that *any* service. The labor class provides virtually all labor for educated expats and nationals: construction and maintenance work, food and hospitality work, domestic help, and shop workers in commercial business operations. They are the people who convert direction into substance and service into a fine art. In many shopping centers, and certainly hotels, an attendant in public restrooms cleans sinks and toilet stalls after each use, right down to folding the end of a toilet-paper roll into a unique geometric configuration. Escalators often have an attendant standing at one end holding a Lysol-saturated cloth against the revolving rubber handrail. White-gloved greeters open doors at hotels, and others serve tea and dates upon entry. It was not unusual at even a midlevel restaurant that our chairs were pulled out for us and scooted back, followed by a cloth napkin being placed on our laps and a lemon- or lime-scented finger bowl provided. My wife and I counted forty-one *Yes, sir*s and *Good evening, madam*s from the moment we exited our vehicle at the valet parking portico at the Shangri-La Resort Hotel until we returned to the car after dinner. The hospitality staff had me convinced that Pamela had changed her name to Madam.

The brains—or white-collar, educated, and skilled people—are the second of the three classes. This group comprises approximately 1.5 million people, or 30 percent of the country's total population. The people in this brain trust and their families are predominantly Arabian, Iranian, and Western expats. They are the master planners, consultants, engineers, architects, and project directors, to name a few, who create and fulfill the dreams of the Rulers. A significant percentage of the Western expats are from the UK. The British ended their protective influence in the UAE in 1968, but its impact and population remains sizable.

Emiratis are the bank. It is their money, their investments, their land, their vision, their rules, and their ultimate decisions that form their country's direction and position its global standing. Interestingly, they make up only 16 percent of their country's population and 3 percent of its workforce, depending on who is keeping tabs.

Emiratization was a widely used buzzword in Abu Dhabi in 2009. A government decree, called a law in the States, was issued to increase the percentage of Abu Dhabi nationals in the workforce by modifying hiring and firing practices. Higher education programs for Emirati students are undergoing changes to become more comprehensive in order to accelerate the integration. Many Westerners anticipate that the rate of progress equates to that of the tortoise in its race with the hare. Emiratis have been afforded a living for the past forty years and have, essentially, not had to work. They are individuals with high net worth, averaging an estimated $17 million per person. No fast rule exists regarding the degree of the government's distribution of wealth to Emiratis, but visual evidence suggests that it is considerable. In addition to receiving a stipend from the government, sizable incentives are often included to encourage nationals to marry nationals and then have large families in an effort to balance the federation's population, which is overwhelmingly composed of expats. Enticements may include a plot of land on which to construct a commercial building, villa, or family compound; an interest-free mortgage or other soft loans; or even a villa.

The neighboring Omanis have a saying: "Omanis work for a living. Emiratis are provided a living." Nationals' motivation to work continues to be slow to emerge. I cannot understand how the government's generous financial contributions are anything but fundamentally counterproductive in erasing the attitude of unemployment supremacy. They are, instead, a perfect recipe for the continuance of a class-based structure.

* *

Chauncey, a neighbor, verbally accosted me from his front porch on the day after we moved into our villa. I had uncoiled a water hose and begun to wash the sand dust off the front porch's marble tiles.

"What do you think you're doing, mate?"

"Washing off my front porch," I said. Duh.

"Indians do that, not a white face!"

I was astonished. My neighbor was a flaming racist! I happen to derive gratification from hosing off a porch or patio. I ignored his racist statement and completed what I had started, an ornery response to his misguided direction.

I soon learned that Chauncey was correct. Most nationals and Westerners would not be caught dead washing their vehicles or boats; watering or tending their gardens; carrying a grocery bag into their villas; hauling garbage; cleaning a villa; washing windows, clothes, or dishes; setting the table; relocating a chaise lounge from one side of a pool to the other; or, oftentimes, even preparing meals or fueling their vehicles. These service expectations define class-based life in the UAE. Raised in England, Chauncey was used to having a service class. Regardless, he was still what I personally construed to be a mild racist.

What Chauncey did not mention was the preparatory work *preceding* my hosing off our villa's front porch. It is not always as simple as it may appear. Garden hoses are sold in Abu Dhabi without the connecting male and female end pieces. The relatively inexpensive plastic or metal repair kits found in Home Depot or Lowes back in the States are nonexistent there. So are Home Depots and Lowes. The options are as follows: (1) purchase Ace Hardware's expensive, metric, noninterchangeable, bright orange, plastic end-adapter kits or (2) leave it to the laborers to create a solution. The carousel display of hose fittings at Ace collects dust. Option 2 is the accepted choice.

A used, white plastic grocery store bag coupled with a short length of rusty baling wire is the universal Band-Aid used to deal with a hose manufactured by the cost-conscious Chinese manufacturer. Connection to a hose bib is a slam dunk. Merely work a raw end of the hose onto the protruding end of the bib and secure it with baling wire. To lengthen a hose requires moxie. Slit the end of one hose and cram the slit end into the end of another hose of the same diameter. Wrap it tightly with a length of plastic torn from a grocery bag and secure it with wire. The work is guaranteed to last a week before it requires a routine change of plastic. Water leaks between the ends of hoses are partially contained with a plastic-bag tourniquet. This lesser-developed-world solution is significantly more cost-effective than Option 1. The irony is that this handiwork is performed in the city with the wealthiest population per capita on the planet.

The Indian ethnic group's welcoming expressions are some of the warmest in the world. A radiant smile and a hand placed across the heart signifies *Thank you* or *It was my pleasure*. An archetypal Indian gesture is the head bobble. Shaking or wiggling the head from side to side two or three times is somewhat equivalent to a Westerner's forward and backward nod. The nonverbal communication has an all-encompassing interpretation: *Hello, you are welcome*, or anything close.

I resolved to try a head bobble on an Indian stranger. When our eyes first met, I offered a little head wiggle and a smile. The result was astounding! The stranger returned an incandescent smile and set to such head waggling that I became a bit alarmed. The message conveyed in that gentle exchange jump-started my elementary-level understanding of nonverbal communication with a Hindi- or Urdu-speaking expat.

My wife's frequent early-morning horseback rides with her female Abu Dhabi equestrian friends are a vivid example of the country's class-based interaction. Royals own the vast majority of the country's private horse farms and stables. They invest considerable sums of money to acquire some of the finest equine stock in the world, as well as breed and raise hundreds of prize horses locally. Many of the larger farms have manicured green pastures similar to fairways at Pebble Beach Golf Links in California and are surrounded by Kentucky horse farm white-rail fencing. Large and impeccably clean stalls with overhead fans, an oval racetrack, a lap pool for exercising horses, and veterinary and dietary facilities are generally standard inventory, and hundreds of stable hands and grooms maintain the highest level of horse care and facility maintenance. Horse poop magically disappears within minutes after hitting the ground.

Back in California, Pamela derived gratification from hands-on work with her horse. The joy that comes from brushing, washing, braiding manes and tails, cleaning hooves, shoeing, vetting, bridling and saddling, walking, training, trailering, feeding, and tactile conversation provides mental therapy. In Abu Dhabi, there is an unspoken protocol. The stable hands, and only they, tend to the horses. Prior to Pamela's arrival at the stable, the animal is washed and dried, hooves are cleaned, mane and tail are combed and often braided, and the horse is tacked up with a polished saddle over a white saddle pad. The Moroccan stable hands, each wearing a proud smile, and the mount's whinny welcome her.

Upon completion of her ride, stable hands remove the saddle and pad, walk the horse back to the "washing machine" prior to its therapeutic swim in the lap pool, and periodically cap off the routine with an upper leg massage. I accompanied Pamela to one stable that was equipped to wash, dry, iron, and return a rider's riding britches post haste should they become soiled or sweaty during the ride. In the interim, the rider may relax in the posh, air-conditioned riding quarters while sipping a freshly squeezed fruit drink served by a tea boy. Pamela casually mentioned to her equestrian soul mates back in the States that her riding expectations have, not by choice, been elevated.

Virtually all vehicles owned by Emiratis and Western expats were washed daily, or as needed, by their Asian housekeeper or staff of housekeepers. I would leave a water bucket, rags, chamois, and an aerosol can of Armor All Tire Foam in an outdoor closet earmarked for their exclusive use. I saw no noticeable difference in the appearance of my Toyota SUV's tires after a month's worth of washings even though I had replaced three empty cans. One evening, I peeked out the villa's entry door to observe a washing. The housekeeper was spraying the tire foam on the polished aluminum wheel, not the rubber tire. Exhibiting my appreciation for his unfailing willingness to please, we shared a laugh while I patiently demonstrated that the product was to be sprayed on the black tire, as depicted by the color picture on the can. I was again reminded never to overlook the fact that we come from different backgrounds and have different interpretations and priorities, none of which are to be taken for granted.

Racial tension has played a role throughout human history. Today's sophisticated Internet technology connects people globally and exposes revolutionary ideals that propel the evolving turmoil in many Middle Eastern and North African (MENA) countries. Each country has a unique set of internal dynamics that sparks unrest for completely different reasons. Personal freedoms, high unemployment, and a future of perceived hopelessness are among the more notable. Hostility is not evident in the ethnically diverse UAE. To the contrary, the de facto caste system appears to be, at least temporarily, a remarkable working example of how people from all ethnicities and walks of life can peacefully coexist when rulers are fair-minded. Results of the distribution of the revenue from the country's enviable trade surplus are also visible. Although the playing field of servitude is elevated, the red flag would never fade to anything lighter than pink for me.

Part Six

Cultural Immersion Vignettes

Brits and Webster

It cannot go unsaid—I have developed an exceptional love and appreciation for Brits. Their presence and influence dominated a huge percentage of my waking hours, socially and professionally, politically and inspirationally, on radio and TV and at rugby matches. Many British friends thought my Californian accent was a pain to comprehend, and my Scottish and Irish colleagues were exceptional critics. But I stood my ground, and they stood theirs. The stubborn standoff formed the basis for laughter, appreciation, trust, and remarkable friendships. Guys are funny that way. That being said, I take this opportunity to share a few digs.

My fourth-grade teacher would have instructed all Brits to don a dunce cap and sit on a stool facing a corner if she had heard their inexcusable inability to *properly* pronounce and spell words in the English language as Mr. Webster intended. The spelling and grammar checker in Microsoft Word supports my adherence to the US version of the dictionary. My laptop, purchased in Abu Dhabi, was apparently set to the version taught by my fourth-grade teacher. *Capitalize* is spelled with a *z*, not an *s*. What could have possibly been going through a Brit's mind in replacing the *k* in *checkered* with a *qu*? Or inserting a *u* in *labor, honor,* and *color* or adding a *t* to *learn*? What triggered American colonists to remove letters from many English words in order to streamline literary work? Granted, Microsoft created two English software versions of spell check, one for the United States and one for the United Kingdom. Webster apparently had a kid brother living in the United Kingdom named Oxford, last name Dictionary. Several months of concentrated effort passed before I grasped the Brit's disregard for Mr. Webster's hard work. During the extended learning curve, Brit colleagues, who outnumbered me fifty to one, were quick to advise: "Americans work too hard. Europeans work smart." No argument ensued. I obligingly switched my spelling and grammar checker to the UK version and became best friends with the kid facing a corner of the classroom.

On my first day on the job, I overheard Jamison (*JI-ma-sen*), a British colleague in an adjacent office, address Solki, a Ukrainian engineer newbie, saying, "Don't git your fokking knickers in a twist, mate. Haven't you learnt whilst you've bean 'ere that I ked a loot?"

I knew right then and there that Jamison was to be avoided at all costs in any future disagreement.

Two days later, Peter (*PEE-tah*) and Chauncey were seated next to me in a conference room. I lobbed a crumpled Post-it toward a waste container, employing a tricky bank shot off the wall—a LeBron James gimme. It missed. I expected a rhetorical American comment like "air ball" or "brick." But no. Chauncey announced, "Marshall your refuse, mate."

No more bank shots.

Milford, one of my jokester office colleagues, flagged me down as I was walking past his villa. "You watch, mate," he smirked, nodding in the direction of his mother. "Me mum will git her truss caught on both me buggie's boot and that shrubbery" (*SHRUB-r-eh*, as heard in *Monty Python*).

Sure enough, the car's trunk lid snagged her dress—*r-r-r-rip*—and the thorny hedge finished the job. That was the first time I heard a British lady cuss in Brit.

A British couple invited us to their villa for dinner and to see David's (*DI-vids*) boat remodel project. "Press the noisy pedal, come over for a barbie, and see me fit-out, mate!" he shouted on his mobile while working on his boat, anchored in waist-deep water off the beach.

David's wife later described the preparation of her simple green salad. "Slice a tomato (*ta-MAH-toe*) over the leaves (*lyves*), dash of oregano (*ore-a-GAN-o*), dice with blue cheese (*chays*), and serve chilled (*shilled*)."

"Spot on," I replied.

Pamela glared at me. She speaks kitchen Brit.

Another British chap and project director for a company constructing an aluminum foundry outside of Dubai shared, "I'm keen on monitoring the contractors' (*con-TRAC-tors*) schedule (*SHED-ju-ol*) on me aluminum (*al-loo-MIN-ee-um*) plant so we're profitable (*pra-FIT-a-ble*)."

It was about this time that I again (*a-GAIN*) mistakenly believed I was bloody well beginning to understand this massacre of the English language—"touch wood." Knock on wood.

The British colonial influence was demonstrated at a Fourth of July celebration hosted by an American couple at their villa. A look of disgust appeared on the faces of several British guests as American revelers struck up a chorus of "Yankee Doodle."

"What's your problem?" one of the Americans asked.

"This obnoxious party represents the loss of another one of our colonies. Our Redcoats were defeated at the hands of your bloody amateur riflemen blokes in Trenton in 1781," stated one of the Brits in typical dry British humor.

At least he had a decent history teacher, I thought but resisted pointing out.

"If they hadn't announced their arrival with a bugle and worn bright red coats that made them ideal targets, they may have been better matched, mate," the American remarked as if to say *How dumb could they be?* "Incidentally, how did you find the tea in your travels to Boston?"

The dig was politely answered with a long swig of John Adams lager.

During the struggle to refine communication skills with British colleagues, I made a conscientious effort to learn how to *walk* acceptably. Brits walk like they drive—on the opposite, or wrong, side of the sidewalk or hallway. It is essential to stride past an approaching Brit on his *right* side in order to avoid a nasty head-on collision. I often flattened myself against the right wall of a hallway because passers-by stubbornly refused to give way. I did not relish the thought of being responsible for a spilled cup of coffee on a stranger's sport coat. Additional caution was employed in using the proper, or left, door of a double-door unit when entering or exiting a commercial building. Oversight could result in bruised knuckles or a bloody nose. Hand-me-down habits from the colonial era are deep-rooted. The clever author of the American expression "got up on the wrong side of the bed" more than likely had Brits in mind. End of digs, my beloved, *insha'Allah.*

Crescent Moon

Insha'Allah is a glorious term that conveys recognition that God is all knowing. If it is his will that an event will happen, it will happen. If it is his will that it will *not* happen, then it will not happen. The nuances of the term had been somewhat puzzling to me until they were clarified at a small, neighborhood laundry shop. After handing a half dozen dress shirts to the Indian shopkeeper one morning to be cleaned, he affirmed, "Shirts ready end of day, *insha'Allah.*"

Okay, I respect that, I thought. The end of the day for shopkeepers in Abu Dhabi is generally around 2300, depending upon—well, who knows what it might or might not be dependent upon. I did not favor driving back to the shop late in the evening if my shirts would not be ready to pick up.

"Can you assure me they will be cleaned and ready to pick up tomorrow morning?"

"'Morrow 'nother day, *insha'Allah*," he replied.

"Whaddaya mean '*insha'Allah*'? Is there a possibility there won't *be* a tomorrow?"

My exposure to, and understanding of, Ramadan occurred three months after my relocation to Abu Dhabi in 2007. It was a cultural high, a rich enlightenment, and a truly exciting time. Leading up to that September 13, I innocently asked Tawfig, one of Pamela's new Bahraini equestrian friends, when Ramadan would begin.

"Sometime next Tuesday."

"What do you mean 'sometime' next Tuesday? Like 11:45 a.m.?" I asked cynically.

"No, no. At precisely the moment the crescent moon disappears."

"Tawfig, astronomers know precisely where and when the moon will rise and set and become new or full years from now! What am I missing?"

"The Moon Sighting Committee makes the call."

"The *who?*"

I have so much more to understand.

Ramadan is the ninth lunar month of the year in which the Qur'an, the holy book of Islam, was prepared for gradual revelation by the angel Gabriel. It was revealed to followers by the Islamic prophet Muhammad, PBUH (acronym for "peace be upon him"), messenger of God (*Allah* in Arabic), in Makkah in the Gregorian year 622. The Qur'an is to Muslims as the Bible is to Christians and the Torah is to Jews.

As a sidebar, the holiest city in the religion of Islam is Makkah. Saudi Arabia officially changed the spelling from *Mecca* in the 1980s after realizing that the Western media and authors were using the word derogatorily, even though, in most cases, the desecration of the name of this holy city was done ignorantly, not deliberately.

Ramadan is a month of fasting, self-discipline, and purification of the heart and soul to help improve a Muslim's character. It is a time to increase awareness of praiseworthy characteristics like charitableness, kindness, generosity, patience, and forgiveness. Fasting, meaning "refrain" in Arabic, begins at the break of dawn and ends at sunset, after which time begins a festive time for the family to enjoy the company of relatives and friends. An estimated 1.5 billion Muslims worldwide practice fasting, one of the five pillars of Islam. In recognition and honor of Prophet Muhammad's revelation, one-thirtieth of the Qur'an is prescribed to be read during evening prayer on each night of Ramadan. Theoretically, if observers adhere to this guideline, the whole Qur'an will have been recited by the end of the lunar month.

In preparation, Muslims, assisted by their domestic help, stock up on groceries prior to the beginning of Ramadan. Stores are as busy as a big European city's train station. Most grocery stores are open until midnight, the time of day that practicing Muslims are awake. It was a kick to watch shoppers, each with a half dozen or more grocery carts (*trolleys* in Brit) lined up at cashier lines prior to Ramadan. Carts are loaded with dishware, glassware, and food staples like bags of dates, twenty-kilo bags of rice from Pakistan, lamb, naan, sweets, and bottled water. Store employees replace emptied pallets of rice with full ones and restock shelves as rapidly as physically possible. Pickup trucks with side panels transport sheep to market and slaughterhouses. Non-Muslim shoppers resort to daytime shopping to avoid the crowds.

A law of economics dictates that the price of a good typically rises as demand strains supply. Anticipating price adjustments, the Rulers announced that adherence to pre-Ramadan food prices would be maintained prior to, and throughout, the month of Ramadan. I wondered if the Rulers could also control their country's annual inflation rate. *That* would be power. The small neighborhood grocery stores did not necessarily comply with the decree, though, because there are too many to regulate, and many of their owners are not Muslim.

As Tawfig had explained, Ramadan ends when the crescent moon is again sighted by the official Moon Sighting Committee. It is celebrated with the festival of Eid al-Fitr, the most important festival in the UAE. Festive meals with family and friends and modest gift-giving to children take place several days of commemoration and gratitude. Of course, *modest* carries a different connotation in Abu Dhabi than it does in most other Muslim locales. Picture nine Christmas mornings wrapped into one.

Now, this is tricky. The Islamic calendar is lunar and is eleven to twelve days shorter than the solar, or Gregorian (non-Islamic), calendar. Consequently, the month of Ramadan moves back each year by eleven to twelve days. Ramadan has fallen, or will fall, within the summer months of June to September, when the desert temperature soars, for the years 2006–2014. I endured the heat during my first year, feeling overwhelmed by the workload. Sane nationals and expats traditionally take leave prior to or following the Ramadan month and travel to cooler climes. Wealthier nationals head to Paris, London, or their own islands, chateaus, or horse farms. Western expats generally head to their homelands sometime during the summer months or vacation somewhere semiexotic in a two-star hotel. School is out, and roadways and workplaces are quiet. Offices operate on skeleton crews and with reduced hours, and business production is significantly compromised. Commercial business hours are curtailed, with many establishments open only in the evenings. Those residents who remain behind later wonder why they did. Water in swimming pools and the Gulf approach 32°C (90°F). Door handles on unshaded vehicles are too hot to touch, and a cheese omelet can be prepared on the hood of a car. My beloved Brits call it the "bonnet of a buggie." The country appears as if it were hit by the Andromeda strain. Tom Bodett has turned off the light.

Melodic Call to Prayer

The Islamic call to prayer, called *adhan*, was, for me, a melodic break in daily routine, although I had no idea what the unintelligible phrases meant. The Arabic sing-song is recited by the caller, or muezzin, at five prescribed times of day. The calls are broadcast throughout each mosque's neighborhood over a speaker system located high on the mosque's minaret(s). The purpose is to summon the faithful to prayer and make available to followers an intelligible summary of Islamic belief. Each muezzin, however, has a unique vocal style; comparing them would be analogous to comparing Little Richard to Johnny Cash or Luciano Pavarotti. Arabic word recognition evolved slowly—*very* slowly—over my three-year residency.

At each call to prayer, the muezzin recites fifteen verses for Sunni or twenty for Shia sects. Roughly translated (from Sunni), the verse imparts:

Allahu Akbar, meaning "God is greatest"
(repeated four times).
I bear witness that there is no deity except God
(repeated four times)

I bear witness that Muhammad is the Messenger of God
(repeated two times)
Come to prayer
(repeated two times)
Come to success
(repeated two times)
God is greater
(repeated two times)
There is no deity except God

Before entering a mosque, Muslims are required to remove their footwear and cleanse their hands and feet in the areas provided for ablution, or washing. According to Islamic tradition, a state of impurity inhibits the performance of one's prayers. Footwear is left outside the mosque, creating a virtual shoe store. Once believers are inside, the *iman* (comparable to a priest, minister, reverend, cleric, and so forth) begins the sermon. By comparison, Christians recite the Lord's Prayer during their church services, and that prayer's rough translation into Arabic sounds as foreign to a Muslim as the verse in Islam's call to prayer does to a Christian. Nevertheless, the dogma in both recitations is meant to evoke peace, love, and generosity and to recognize an almighty deity.

Purity and Discipline

Khalid, an Emirati friend, introduced me to his wife, Bayan, and two young sons, Hamdan and Hazza. Bayan wore the traditional black abaya and a black, jewel-encrusted shaylah, or headscarf, leaving her face uncovered. She was a beautiful Arabic lady with large, black eyes highlighted in black kohl eyeliner. I knew *not* to say, "Khalid, your wife is gorgeous." His response, spoken or not, would likely be, "Why are you checking out my wife?" My compliment was instead worded, "You have a beautiful family, Khalid."

"And you have beautiful eyes" was his appreciative and most sincere reply. With that, he expressed his recognition of my nonspecific tribute to his entire family, including himself.

On another occasion, tears rolled down from under the black sunglasses of Ali, another Emirati friend, who was standing next to me and speaking on his mobile. I was witnessing a rare public display of emotion by an Emirati male. Out of respect, I offered to excuse myself to allow him some privacy. He gently placed his hand on my arm to indicate that he preferred that I remain next to him. After dropping his mobile back into a side pocket of his kandoura, he blinked a couple of times and said, "Tears are colorless. They ooze out in pleasure and pain, but they reveal the shades. A favorite niece just graduated from girls school, and I am touched."

As I looked deep into Ali's glassy eyes through his barely transparent sunglasses and nodded, he recognized that I shared his pride. His poetic description of the moment was his respectful way of remaining reserved, in spite of being overwhelmed with joy over the academic achievement of a close family member. A high five or jumping chest bump would have been an inappropriate, even an indecent, response in his culture. In Islam, decency is timeless.

Islam also prescribes modesty in dress and actions to preserve dignity and respect between men and women in society. The style of clothing has remained fixed and standardized to establish a sense of equality regardless of perceived social status. It allows men and women to go about their daily lives as contributing members of society, without issues of sexuality becoming a distraction. The Qur'an commands both men and women to be modest and "lower their eyes" when in the presence of each other to help retain politeness and honor. This does not mean that Muslims, or *anyone*, have to walk around looking at the ground. They should merely restrain their glances and not look at each other in a longing way. Lowering a gaze is a sign of respect.

Islam forbids any tight, transparent, or extravagant apparel from being worn in public because it may lead to an improper or suspicious advance. Muslims are not subject to the whimsical fashion industry. To the contrary, their attire is ostentatious in its lack of ostentation. This standard of modesty, established by Allah, may be considered outdated or conservative to Westerners, but not to a Muslim. Many Muslim women believe that modest dress allows them to be recognized for their minds and hearts, not judged by their perceived beauty or lack thereof. Tell *that* to Lady Gaga.

On the Arabian Peninsula, it is customary for men to wear a white covering and women to wear black, all of which, at first glance, appear to originate from the same design shop. Emirati men are most often seen dressed in a white *kandoura*, also called a *dishdash*, which is a full-length, heavy-cotton, long-sleeved, shapeless robe. A white or red-and-white-patterned cotton head scarf, or *ghutrah*, is worn topped by a black *aqal*, a double-circle, woven band. Historically, the *aqal* was used by the Bedu to hobble or handcuff a camel's feet to prevent it from wandering. The headpiece is losing its prominence today as young men drape their ghutrah in creative ways. Large, dark sunglasses, sandals, a wristwatch, and a mobile complete the male attire.

Although the Qur'an makes no reference to color or style, Emirati women commonly wear a black abaya, a loose, elegant article of clothing that covers a woman's body from her shoulders to the floor. A shaylah or *niqab*, a black head scarf, covers her neck and hair, which is held up above the neck with a hair clip. Although a shaylah appears on first glance to be a simple square of black silk material, it often incorporates fashionable, yet subtle, design statements that may include beautiful embroidered patterns and jewels. Many modern-day Emirati women believe that face veiling exceeds minimum dress codes, but it is respected as the choice or cultural norm for others. Those who practice it do not consider it a sign of a woman's inferiority. A *burqa* covers the entire body, except for a slit for the eyes, to prevent skin exposure in public. It is primarily worn by women of the older generation. And, like the men, Emirati women commonly wear large, black sunglasses to further maintain modesty.

In the privacy of the home, or in the presence of only family members and close female friends, Emirati women are free to remove their head coverings and outer garments and adorn themselves with stylish clothing and jewelry. Prada, Givenchy, and Tiffany's appreciate their patronage. As a nonfamily member, it was a rare honor that I was included in a national's family gathering that included Muslim women. Pamela, on the other hand, was a frequent non-Muslim, Western guest.

Two American friends joined me for an evening of entertainment at one of Abu Dhabi's many Western nightclubs. A popular jazz group was on tap, and the club was expecting a sizable crowd. The bouncer at the entrance politely informed us that the club did not permit men to wear sandals inside or women to wear scarves covering their heads. One of my friends was wearing sandals. That, we could handle. But the dress code was evidently discriminatory to those of Muslim faith. Granted, UAE nationals generally do not party in public anyway. They are private individuals, and Islam frowns on dancing, consumption of alcoholic beverages, and public displays of affection. What I failed to understand was that the nightclub's policy is the nationals' discreet way of discouraging indulgence. The three of us stepped to one side of the entry doors, where I removed my socks and handed them to our obstreperous friend, who reluctantly slipped them on under his sandals. We were granted entry. Once inside, I was tempted to ask management what section, paragraph, and rule sanctioned its prejudicial treatment but was reluctant to have my pals wash my mouth out with soap. I confessed that my issue was not an issue. Islamic principles are to be respected, and that is that.

Back in California, I have become accustomed to seeing individuals who have tattooed their bodies to look like a coloring book, possibly to recall a former girlfriend's or boyfriend's name or astrological sign, and pierced their bodies with adornments like pushpins in a corkboard. Moderate Islam tends to tolerate conservative tattoos and body piercings, while stricter interpretations of the faith, as practiced in Abu Dhabi, tend to ban it. Henna painting on a woman's body, commonly seen on hands, is considered acceptable because it wears off. Men are not permitted to have body piercing, although women may have each ear pierced once. In the Muslim faith, any deformation of the body, Allah's creation, is thought to be a sin. Living there, I enjoyed a good relationship with Muslims by learning to respect and to not abuse Islamic customs.

Non-Muslim men and women are not expected to wear traditional Arabic dress in public, but they are encouraged to keep their skin covered and respect the morals of the Muslim country. In a public place, I willingly wore a long-sleeved shirt and full-length pants, and Pamela wore a long-sleeved blouse and soft skirt, dress, or pants for comfort and practicality in the hot climate. Casual Western wear—shorts and a T-shirt or short skirt and a sleeveless blouse—is tolerated when not in a public place. Neighboring Dubai is an exception. It attracts more international tourists, which keeps its clothing styles comparatively trendy and eclectic, often leaning toward a liberal persuasion. Tourists don their native beachwear at beachfront hotels, although women chance getting a fine or a one-way airline ticket out of the country if caught topless or wearing a thong. Expat residents and visiting nonresidents are visitors in a Muslim country. When in Rome, do as the Romans do.

Clothing, regardless of who is wearing it or where it is worn, has drawbacks. A burqa compromises vision. I observed an older lady dressed in a burqa pushing a baby stroller down an aisle in a Carrefour grocery store. The young child strapped into it was screaming, kicking, and flailing his arms. The lady leaned over and attempted to shove a rubber pacifier in the child's mouth, but she repeatedly missed the target. The exasperated kid jerked his head back and forth, desperately trying to snag the pacifier. I felt utterly helpless and wondered on how many other occasions the covered lady's restricted vision proved to be a handicap.

Possibly because Halloween originated with the Celts in England, it remains a special annual day for the many Brits in Abu Dhabi. Parents of Emirati children are challenged to create a costume for a child dressed in traditional attire. I had never before seen Zorro, Tinker Bell, Captain Jack Sparrow, or Harry Potter dressed in a kandoura or an abaya. A rubber, pull-over mask of Frankenstein's monster or some other grotesque figure was an easy cop-out. We were deluged with over one hundred young trick-or-treaters at the door of our villa in our first year. More would have knocked had we not turned off the front porch light when the bowl of miniature Hershey bars was depleted. All of the young children were well-mannered, and most were escorted by their nannies or housekeepers. There were no candy grabbers, kids carrying pillowcases, older kids, or repeats. Tradition calls for children to tell a joke as their trick, our treat. For example, "Do you know what a frog drinks? Croaka-cola."

Two of our equestrian friends announced their plan to get married. When the big day arrived, they exchanged marriage vows in a Christian church. Following the formal ceremony, the wedding party and guests drove out into the desert in four-wheel-drive vehicles to a serene location atop a sand dune with a view of the setting sun and rising moon. The groom and best man were dressed in their formal Scottish kilts. Still dressed to the nines, we expats removed our dress shoes to avoid the impracticality of walking ankle deep in the soft sand. We were a hilarious sight. The Emirati guests were amused by the evidence of how much more sensible sandals were in the desert. While sipping champagne and being treated to a fire-red sunset accentuated by the desert dust, entertainment was provided by an Emirati horseman friend of the bride and groom. One of his renowned Arabian show horses performed show-business-style stunts. It was a wedding to remember.

The proud announcement of an Arabic wedding engagement is a wondrous visual statement, difficult to miss. Strings and strings of brilliant white lights, brighter than Christmas tree lights, are draped from the roof of the bride's family's two- or three-story villa to the ground. The neighborhood may remain illuminated for a week. The generous plots of land allow ample room for the honored families to set up large white tents adjacent to their villas for the male relatives and male friends to gather in privacy. When not playing outdoors, the younger boys and girls are always welcome in either the family villa or the tent throughout the celebratory week. The traditional use of tents is a carryover from the ancient tribal past.

Clean and Cleaner

Emiratis traditionally place generosity above most any other virtue. I quickly recognized that mindful attention to their traditional protocol demonstrated my appreciation and gratitude. Emirati friends introduced me to a modified Western world of etiquette influenced by cleanliness. The left hand of the human body is considered to be less pure than the right. I presumed I was blessed, being right-handed. Items, particularly food-related, are handed to or received by another person using the right hand. If the item is large or heavy and requires two hands, the left hand may be placed underneath the item, under the right hand, or supporting the wrist but not in contact with the other person. Likewise, the left hand should not be used when eating or helping oneself to food from a plate or a bowl. My learning curve was shortened by sitting on my left hand. Business etiquette includes a comparable protocol. Shaking hands or exchanging paperwork, including business cards, is done with the right hand. Among Muslims, the left hand is reserved for bodily hygiene.

At first, I found it to be a hassle that a straw is placed in the can, bottle, or glass of *all* soft drinks, exotic drinks, and water served at restaurants in the UAE except those with dollar signs all over the menu. Back in the States, I believed my invincibility to germs validated setting the straw on the table before sipping a drink. Muslim culture, and Western to a lesser degree, is strict about cleanliness regarding an object that comes in contact with the skin. The rim of a glass, the top of an aluminum can, and the cap on a screw-top bottle are targets for harmful bacteria. Canned and bottled beverages are opened in front of customers with care to avoid touching any areas unnecessarily. Paper towel dispensers in public restrooms are oftentimes nonexistent because of potential contamination. Electric warm-air blowers are the preferred substitute.

As a child, I was taught to offer a firm handshake to a stranger when introduced, but the exchange of greetings between an Emirati Muslim and a non-Muslim is initiated by the Muslim only if he or she chooses to make contact with the non-Muslim's hand. It was mutually awkward when I neglected to follow a lead and, out of Western habit, thrust my hand out and crunched the hand of an unsuspecting Muslim. I learned to observe cues and be prepared to avoid any contact at all. Close male Emirati Muslim friends and relatives often greet each other by touching noses. No kiss. No hug. Close female Muslim friends and relatives acknowledge one another with a warm smile and possibly a gentle hand or finger touch. Islam discourages public displays of affection between people of the opposite gender, including activities as minor as hand-holding between married people.

If a dog or cat happened to reside in the villa or compound of an Emirati, I never noticed. Animals are considered unclean, even if they have completed a thorough tongue bath. Muslims cleanse their hands, if possible, if they intentionally or inadvertently come in contact with an animal. Pigs must not be touched or eaten, a tradition dating back to Abraham. It is written in the Qur'an: "Forbidden to you are: dead meat, blood, the flesh of swine…." Then, Leviticus 11:7–8 says, "Of their flesh shall ye not eat, and their carcass shall ye not touch; they are unclean to you." Interestingly, chemical analysis of a pig's blood shows that it contains an abundance of uric acid, a chemical substance that can be injurious to human health. Medical science has found that pigs pose a risk of human exposure to various diseases because the pig is host to many parasites and because its biochemistry excretes only 2 percent of its total uric acid content. The remaining 98 percent remains in the body. Not to be ignored is the fact that pigs eat anything and everything on the ground.

As non-Muslims, we were able to purchase pork chops, ham, bacon, sausage, and other forms of pork in specialty grocery stores— Spinney's being the most popular—without being disrespectful. The meat is obscured in a refrigerated room in a rear corner of the store and accessed through clear, thick plastic panels suspended from the ceiling. *But*, pork is thoroughly cooked before eaten. Out of deference to Islamic belief, I felt uncomfortable viewing rear-lighted pictures of various *ham*burgers above the ordering counter in fast-food restaurants throughout Abu Dhabi and Dubai. Although hamburgers do not incorporate pork, "Big Mac," "Whopper," and simply "burger and fries" sound a bit less contaminated.

Passions and Pastimes
Being an accredited sports freak, I quickly learnt (heh heh) that cricket, rugby, and soccer, called football, are the European, Asian, African, Australian, and South American versions of American baseball, basketball, and football entertainment. The three participation sports are played with equal passion in world-class stadiums by all ethnic groups. Emiratis, on the other hand, love their horse and camel racing and falconry.

Cricket is fanatically followed by half of the world's population, but the game is rarely mentioned in the sports section of any US newspaper. If it were, I venture to guess that 95 percent of readers wouldn't have the foggiest idea of how the game is played. That includes me. In the cooler hours bordering sunset, sandlot (maybe this is where the term originated) pickup cricket games are frequently played by people from Pakistani, Indian, and North African migrant ethnic groups. The bats and wickets are generally salvaged from discarded construction lumber. During playing season, a minimum of two full pages of print and pictures are regularly dedicated to cricket in the English versions of the *Gulf News*, *Khaleej Times*, and the *National*.

Pakistan beat Sri Lanka by 10 wickets. After playing a lone hand, Sidique blasted 1 off 49 balls but the Sri Lankans were bowled for 140 in 19.4 overs. In another game, India was bundled out for 76 in the first innings by South Africa, losing 10 wickets in 20 overs. India did not play its premier spinner bowler.

What the sports reporter failed to mention is that the games could span five days!

Camel polo is a colorful example of creatively stretching what is readily at hand. Picture two riders on a camel—one driver and one polo-stick whacker. Camels' behavior is unpredictable. Their movements appear svelte, but their gallop is comparable to a dinghy ride in a rough sea. The gangly-looking beast may unexpectedly squat on all fours during play, close his gorgeous eyes, and lose interest for a time to be determined only by him. Once he regains his nerve, the haughty creature may choose to rise and rejoin the fun with the whacker continuing to swing a stick between his legs. There is not a camel on Earth that envisioned that life following his teenage years roaming the desert would be spent playing polo on a manicured grass polo field.

The world's biggest (what else is new in Abu Dhabi and Dubai?) camel and hybrid falcon auction and saluki beauty contest are combined into a consistently well-attended, annual event in Abu Dhabi. In 2009, eight hundred camel owners converged in Abu Dhabi with a total of twenty thousand camels. A panel of experts judged the camels based on their physical attributes, including their long eyelashes and necklines. Because the camel is a treasured part of Arabic heritage, the auction draws Emirati men who inspect, haggle, and barter on the prized creatures as if they were the *Mona Lisa*. Top camels often sell for upward of $250,000. A *non*pedigree camel might be sold for the cost of a Toyota.

Prize beauty contest contestant

The falcon and Arabian horse are part of the Emirati heritage

The falcon is the country's national bird, and hunting with falcons is a national pastime. It is difficult to overestimate the importance of falconry in the UAE. Practiced in the Arabian Gulf for four thousand years, it represents the values, traditions, and heritage of the Emirates. Falconry was an integral part of desert life, and its prey supplemented the Bedouin diet with meat such as hare and the houbara bird. A diet of small desert rodents and birds meets the falcon's recommended daily requirements. Today, many of the farms owned by Royals include a sophisticated falcon facility to breed, incubate, raise, and train their prized birds. Dedicated falconers often make an annual hunting pilgrimage to Pakistan with three or four of their top birds of prey. The UAE's government logo is the distinguished falcon, and its image is found on banknotes, vehicle license plates, planes of the national airlines, signage, and clothing and has even been incorporated into colorful landscape design work.

I once watched a teenage Emirati boy fly his peregrine falcon at dusk among the red desert dunes outside of Abu Dhabi. Later, sitting together on the sand, he explained quite articulately (according to my rough recollection),

Emiratis believe that the falcon brings, through his manners and his nature, everyone from Ruler to the common man to the same level—his level. Man might possess far greater intelligence, but the falcon can fly; he can outmaneuver us, and he sees, hears, and smells better than us. He does not adapt to accept us. He does not need to. Instead, for the honor of his company, we must do as he wishes and respect his authority. At all times, the falconer must be positive, not negative, in training his falcon. This training establishes the falconer's benchmark for nurturing his children.

Wow! Where did this gem of a kid come from?

Mature, majestic gyrfalcons, saker falcons, and peregrine falcons often draw ten to twenty-five thousand dollars at auction. The proceeds generated go toward the protection of endangered falcons and camel research. Falcon protection is understandable, but camel research? If you can tolerate a camel's unpleasant body odor and its creepy ability to spit at someone it ascertains to be obstreperous, it makes an ideal house pet—assuming the house has no walls and sits on a hectare of sand. According to the camel census office (truly), there were 378,000 camels in the emirate of Abu Dhabi alone in 2010.

A more traditional house pet, the saluki dog is a sleek cousin of the greyhound and a superb candidate to impress the timers at the Bonneville Salt Flats in Utah. I accompanied a proud saluki owner while she "walked" her three fleet, blonde-haired dogs in the scrub-brush desert behind her villa. Never have I seen dogs sprint as fast as her pets. Even though the cheetah holds the speed record for four-legged animals, I walked away believing it would have its paws full if a saluki were to challenge it to a race. The speedster, known for its exceptional stamina and intelligence, has adapted to the harsh desert existence and is bred to be a hunting dog. The prestigious annual saluki beauty contest appeared to be difficult to judge because the creatures, by nature, in my opinion, look as if they could each comfortably consume a forty-kilo (approximately twenty pound) bag of dog food. However, the prized animals are lovable, loyal, clean, and mild-mannered.

The Rulers of the seven emirates have set aside land for many private wild-animal preserves to ensure the maintenance of indigenous animal populations in spite of the country's rapid growth. I was surprised and pleased to discover that the San Diego Wild Animal Park in California is affiliated with Al Ain's relatively new zoo, the largest in the UAE. Al Ain is the second-largest city in the emirate of Abu Dhabi, nestled "high" (300 meters, or 984 feet) in the red sand dunes 160 kilometers (96 miles) east of Abu Dhabi city on the Omani border. Known as the Garden City because of its many oases, it has been continuously inhabited for more than four thousand years and is central to the country's cultural heritage. Today, Al Ain has the country's highest number of nationals and is the birthplace of Sheikh Zayed, revered founder of the UAE.

Part Seven

———◆◆◆———

Meanwhile, Back on Yas Island

Yas Marina was designed to be located *within* the island, or sandbar, not attached to its periphery. A momentous quantity of sand, estimated at 1.2 million cubic meters (1.57 million cubic yards), would first have to be excavated and a perimeter wall of concrete key-blocks (each block weighing twenty tons) completed before the strip of land connecting the marina entrance to the waterway could be removed in order to flood the dry marina. The time-consuming assembly of the enormous floating docks, called pontoons, would then commence. My work was cut out, and expectations were sky-high. The project development team had to make every moment count. I figured that if my colleagues were fearless and found no task too daunting, then so would I.

Shortly after ground was broken on the marina project, I was sharing my excitement with several colleagues at the end of a day in the open-air cocktail lounge at Pearls & Caviar, a fashionable disco hot spot. Its open-air, second-story deck offers a mesmerizing view of the majestic Grand Mosque—the Notre Dame of Islam—across the waterway that separates Abu Dhabi island from the mainland. Unbeknownst to me, a member of the Royal Family and his contingent of cronies occupied an adjacent, spacious seating area. A genteel waiter informed me that my presence was requested there.

I glanced over my shoulder, recognized the Sheikh, and figured he must know who I am. He appeared relaxed, even gentle. Upon my arrival, he smiled and said, "I have been told you know how to build a five-star marina."

"Yes, sir. I do."

"It pleases me to hear you confirm that. Make Yas a *six*-star."

His smile, piercing eye contact, and hesitation waiting for my acknowledgement were indelible. I smiled and nodded slightly. *It will be done.* No handshake was exchanged. The prestige conveyed by a high "star" ranking is of utmost importance to the Rulers of Abu Dhabi (and Dubai), significantly more so than in other emerging, or emerged, nations.

Think Big

The demand for ever-larger luxury yachts has grown exponentially since the mid-1990s. The growth has been fueled especially by the Middle Eastern and Russian markets. As of March 2011, seven of the world's ten largest superyachts and an estimated thirty of the top one hundred were owned by wealthy Middle Easterners. The numbers are estimated because many owners choose to remain anonymous. When I arrived in Abu Dhabi in 2007, the rulers of the oil-rich countries—UAE, Qatar, Kuwait, Oman, and Saudi Arabia—were accumulating megayachts with one-upsmanship regularity, and few of their luxury yachts were berthed in the Arabian Gulf. The Mediterranean and Caribbean were the favored cruising grounds. My aim was to develop a reason to alter the trend.

As the company's head of marinas, my primary focus was to develop top-notch marinas that would attract and be capable of berthing many of these megayachts, as well as those owned by non–Middle Easterners. Yas Marina would be the first marina to be completed, and Abu Dhabi's Royal Family's luxury yachts would be the first to occupy it. And next door, the Ruler of Dubai, HH

Sheikh Mohammad bin Rashid Al Maktoum, owns one of the—if not *the*—largest private superyachts in the world (as of 2010). A shroud of secrecy prevails at the top end of the roll call. *Dubai*, completed in 2006, is 162 meters (532 feet), or 1.7 football fields, long. Stated differently, she is as long as thirty-five Lamborghinis lined up end to end and well over twenty-five times their total cost, excluding her Sikorsky S76 helicopter. Would Dubai's Ruler expect an accommodation for his floating palace in Yas Marina? Who would tell him, "Sorry, she won't fit. Take her to a commercial port"?

The $125 million Yas Marina and quay in the channel immediately outside the entrance to the marina were designed to handle 146 yachts up to 100 meters (325 feet) long, always with exceptions. For comparison, a multi-billion-dollar Los Angeles class nuclear submarine is 353 feet long. Yas Marina is to date the most high-tech marina facility ever constructed. The F1 racetrack wraps around five sides of the fifteen-sided marina and provides yacht owners and their guests with an unobstructed view of much of the race. Monaco offers a somewhat similar racetrack configuration on its public streets adjacent to its marina, although the view from a luxury yacht is comparatively obstructed.

Top on my list at the onset of construction was to ensure that this luxury yacht marina would have sufficient electrical capacity to power the air-conditioning, spas, swimming pools, theaters, gourmet galleys, elevators, and abundant state-of-the-art lighting and electronics on the megayachts, assuming that every yacht in the marina would have them running concurrently. The outrageous number of kilowatts is capable of powering a midsize city—similar to the power consumption at Ski Dubai. Continuous blue strip-lighting would be installed around the 3,800-meter (2.3-mile) perimeter of the floating pontoons to illuminate the water at night, and a high-volume vacuum waste management system would be installed to evacuate the tremendous quantity of refuse generated by megayachts via underground pipelines to a processing facility 1.5 kilometers (0.9 miles) away. Helicopter pads and limousine and concierge service to transport owners and their guests to yachts via golf cart (*buggie* in Brit-speak) or yacht tender would be provided. Fine food provisioning would be offered by both upscale marina restaurants, also under construction, and a high-exposure parking lot for luxury vehicles— Rolls, Maybach, Bentley, Aston Martin, Maserati, Lamborghini, Ferrari, Porsche, and Mercedes, to name most—would be situated adjacent to the longest berths. The marina staff would be trained to provide six-star service, and they would dress the part. Hired security personnel would supplement the professional security presence that often accompanies a high-profile luxury yacht.

Fred, the newest member on the marina team, was well entrenched working with government agencies on waterway rules and guidelines for pleasure boaters. At the same time, the military was formulating every precautionary measure to ensure that the inaugural F1 race week would take place without incident. The Rulers anticipated that members of their extended families and many international heads of state, dignitaries, and celebrities would attend. Security was critical. A highly visible military presence would protect the waterways, both on the surface and underwater, as well as the surrounding airspace and the island itself. Although not announced, it was rumored that provisions would include divers to check the bottoms of yachts for explosive devices prior to their entrance to the marina. The last thing the Rulers, or *any* peace-loving individual, wanted to experience in the UAE was a terrorist attack. The worldwide implications resulting from an attempted assassination would be unfathomable.

At the inception of Yas Marina's construction, I raised the question with a project director whether the air draught, or clearance, under the highest point of the Saadiyat Bridge, which was concurrently under construction, would be sufficient for a superyacht. The ten-lane bridge spans the one-kilometer-wide waterway, connecting Abu Dhabi island to Saadiyat Island, which, in turn, connects to Yas Island, and a vessel must cruise underneath the bridge on its way to and from Yas Marina. My inquiry traveled at the speed of light right to the top. The Sheikhs wanted assurance that their yachts would be able to cruise unimpeded to Yas Marina. I was tasked with providing a list of the heights above the waterline of *all* megayachts within two days. Height is the one measurement that is *not* recorded in Lloyd's Registry of Yachts because the superstructure on the top of large yachts is frequently modified as technology changes or whimsy strikes. *No task is too daunting.* I called a dozen companies around the world that build megayachts only to be told by their respective executives that height is classified information. Using a ruler, I scaled the heights of the largest luxury yachts where possible from pictures in yacht brochures. A couple of the monstrous yachts would not clear the bridge. The Rulers entertained the idea of raising the height of the nearly completed concrete bridge another few meters to accommodate their yachting brethren. By doing so, however, the added construction time would extend the project's completion past the entire Yas project's inflexible deadline. That was unacceptable. Vehicle access to the island was equally as vital as boat traffic, if not more so. Instead, the decision was made to alert the captains of all yachts to the clearance restrictions so they would be independently responsible for their yachts' safe passage.

Periodically, a red lightbulb would illuminate in my head while reviewing any and every issue that a yacht captain might encounter while cruising to or maneuvering within Yas Marina. I asked the captain of a megayacht owned by a sheikh to critique my punch list to ensure that I had the bases covered. At that time, the number of luxury yachts that would ultimately visit the marina and their lengths were unknown. The lightbulb exploded. The waterway outside the marina was only 150 meters (165 yards) wide, although it *appeared* to be wider and *appeared* to provide adequate room to spin a megayacht 180 degrees. The captain's authoritative reply was disheartening: "Any yacht longer than 100 meters cannot safely maneuver in a 150-meter-wide channel. Wind and current can be unforgiving. Other traffic, including emergency watercraft, must be considered. I require at least one and a half boat lengths of clear water before I'll consider piloting a yacht in tight quarters."

My breathing stopped, and I felt the blood begin to drain from my head. I envisioned an upset Sheikh. *Heads will roll like coconuts*, I thought, *including mine*. "I've got a [expletive] problem," I muttered to the captain. "The channel needs to be widened in front of the marina." I knew that the time and cost to resolve the predicament would be cheap insurance.

My directions were implicit: *Make it six-star*. The word *no* is not to be in my vocabulary. My head was ringing. The clock was running. To downright compound matters, one of Sheikh Zayed's immense palaces sat at the water's edge across the channel from the marina—precisely where the channel would have to be widened. Yikes! Granted, it had sat there unoccupied for years. I was told that even though the exterior of the white palace was finished, the interior was not. Does it matter? Who makes the decision to demolish a palace owned by the founder of the country? The hot potato could be handled only by the President and the Crown Prince of Abu Dhabi, two of Sheikh Zayed's sons. I figured it was at least fortunate that each of those Rulers owned a large luxury yacht. After considerable time-consuming, behind-the-scenes mediation by members of the Royal Family, the decision was handed down to demolish the palace. Ornate windows, hardwood doors, and stunning interior moldings were salvaged by the demolition company. Rumors surfaced that gold leaf was even chipped from ceilings. It was painful to view the grand structure's swift annihilation, recognizing that it had required years to construct.

The engineering team designed a "turning basin" that would meet the maneuvering requirements of the largest yachts expected to cruise to the marina. Heavy equipment and a dredger were imported to excavate an immense concave chunk of land (sand) from the opposite side of the channel. Close to 1.5 million cubic meters (just shy of 2 million cubic yards) of material, three hundred thousand cubic meters more than were removed for the giant marina itself, were excavated within three months at a cost of $9.3 million. The price tag of the playground for big boys' toys was growing exponentially, and the list of remarkable feats was lengthening.

* *

Throughout my ongoing work assembling the company's marina portfolio, I crossed paths with some extraordinarily colorful heavy-hitters. One such individual was the warm and gracious Greek tycoon Andreas Liveras. In 2008, he brought two of his charter fleet's superyachts, the 85-meter (279-foot) *Alysia* and the 90-meter (295-foot) *Lauren L*, to Abu Dhabi for a winter layover. They were the largest chartered yachts to ever grace Abu Dhabi's waters. Each luxurious yacht could easily entertain two hundred guests in seven-star indulgence. They provided an exclusive retreat for Andreas and his family and friends at any global port at which they chose to anchor.

My wife wrote an article about *Alysia* for the 2009 January–February issue of *Yachts Emirates*, a glossy international yachting magazine published in Dubai. The article was submitted to the magazine the day *Alysia* departed Abu Dhabi for a brief stay in Mumbai, India, en route to the Maldives, with Andreas on board. Two days later, Andreas was among the 164 people killed in the Pakistani-based terrorist attacks across Mumbai. He and *Alysia*'s cruise director were dining at the Taj Mahal Palace Hotel at the time. The amended last paragraph in Pamela's article was an emotional condolence to his family, friends, and many colleagues in the yachting industry. I was shaken. Andreas's murder was a sober reminder that we lived in a tumultuous region of the world.

Alysia was sold in 2010 to an Abu Dhabi sheikh for a purported $100 million.

Soon after my hire in Abu Dhabi, an opportunity arose to speak briefly with a member of the government's Executive Council at the conclusion of a conference at the $3 billion Emirates Palace. I complimented him on the dedication and tenacity that he and others within the government had demonstrated in establishing remarkably high benchmarks for the country and its people. His momentary silence suggested that he had heard that line many times before. Looking me straight in the eyes, he spoke from his heart. "I am an ordinary man, but you have perceived me as an enlightened person. I have to work hard to live up to that image. You have given me additional responsibility."

His extraordinary eloquence and humility left me speechless as he nodded and continued his exit past me, encircled by his protective contingent. It was evident to me why Emiratis revere their leaders.

Another encounter appeared at first to be a fairy tale—a scandalous one that might be divulged at a casual social gathering by a self-important individual. My eyes and ears confirmed otherwise. The company flew me to Monaco for the annual, principality-hosted Formula One race. My assignment was to refine my comprehension of how to dovetail a high-end marina and an F1 race into a single, flawless, world-class extravaganza. On the final day of my four-day research project, I was engrossed in a conversation with the captain of a megayacht that was berthed in Monaco's yacht harbor. While seated on one of the rear decks of the magnificent vessel and overlooking the crowd of people who were strolling along the dock below and gawking at the opulent yachts, a gentleman dressed in a stylish black suit bullied his way past the uniformed crewmember who was standing at the foot of the gangway, monitoring access to the yacht. Once up the gangway, and without an introduction, he brazenly asked the captain if he would show him around the boat. I recognized a Russian accent. The captain reluctantly obliged, although the megayacht was not open for public viewing. When they returned thirty minutes later to where I was seated, the guest stated that he wanted to buy the yacht. The captain assumed he was kidding, judging from his expression. He was not. The Russian insisted that the captain locate the yacht's owner on his mobile and request that he return so that he could converse with him directly and privately. The owner was out of the country, so the captain called him on a mobile phone. Fifteen minutes of loud negotiations ensued in the interior salon between the Russian and the owner, after which the Russian returned to the rear deck and handed the mobile back to the captain to terminate the call with the owner. The captain had a look of disbelief on his face. The brash Russian waved a hand to get the attention of two other dark-suited men standing on the dock. One of them was holding a black valise that was chained to his wrist. Once aboard, he placed the leather suitcase on the table in front of me, removed its chain, entered the combination, and opened the lid, facing the wide-eyed captain of the yacht. *It was not a fairy tale!* The suitcase was completely filled with packets of paper currency. I was too blown away to observe whether the notes were in dollars, euros, pounds, or rubles, but I *did* know that it was not monopoly money. I somehow retained a poker-faced look of boredom even though my heart was beating loud enough to create ripples on the water in the marina. The Russian oligarch had just purchased a yacht valued in the neighborhood of $40 million, the transaction was consummated in under an hour, and he already had two bodyguards onboard.

Beacons of Eminence

What a thrill it was to rise early every morning with anticipation and vigor, prepared to take on Goliath, and with the knowledge that the caliber of the project on which I was working was unparalleled. The completed marina would treat the owners and their guests on the finest private yachts on the planet to a level of indulgence never before experienced. Money flowed as if from a wide-open hose bib. It was next to impossible to feel guilty about the stream of dirham because uncompromising expectations were instilled in the entire team of talented expats on the workforce.

A world-class marina, I believed, deserved a world-class yacht club. A yacht club would provide a nautical retreat for its exclusive clientele and possibly offer reciprocal privileges to members of the most prestigious yacht clubs in the world. The Monaco Yacht Club would be first on my hit hist. No sooner had I presented my plan to the company's CEO than a world-renowned architectural firm was hired and provided free rein to create a unique structure that would capture the Rulers' vision—the boundaries of which were nonexistent—and deliver another statement of eminence for the Yas Island project. Our nonnegotiable time schedule to complete the entire megaproject now stood at twenty-two months. I did not care to imagine the unspecified repercussions for not completing the yacht club within the deadline. Through the will of Allah, the lead architect submitted his preliminaries in record time. When I first viewed the drawings, I was shocked. They were not at all what I had had in mind. I anticipated a futuristic facade, but this looked like a slick UFO. The architect proclaimed that the immense three-story structure, with its forty-five-meter (147-foot) observation tower, somewhat resembled the beak of a falcon, the country's national bird. To no one's surprise, the Rulers approved the yacht club's conceptual drawings, and ground was immediately broken on the site that

I had earmarked at the entrance to the marina. A plan review, building permit, and municipal inspections were not necessary. The architectural firm was tops, the contractor was a proven entity, and government "financing" was as good as gold—or oil. What more could a team of project directors ask for?

The iconic Yas Marina Yacht Club, the first yacht club built in the emirate, is a $105 million work of modern art and the most expensive yacht club on the globe. At night, the building is illuminated internally and externally with an envelope of lighting comprised of LEDs that are designed to convert its shell into a giant viewing screen. But no matter how many times and from what angle I viewed this building during its construction, I could never make out its resemblance to a bird.

Yas Marina Yacht Club

Because the decision to build the yacht club came as the concrete perimeter walls of the marina and the adjacent racetrack were nearing completion, adequate parking had not been factored into the overall footprint to accommodate the club's future patrons. A five-star restaurant and a nightclub with large seating capacities would be two of the several lessees. The unique water and landscape features leading up to the yacht club's spacious chauffeur and valet drop-off and pickup area consumed a large chunk of land. I provided to the master planners and architect my estimate of vehicle spaces that would be required to service patrons of the marina and the yacht club during a Formula One race week. Within two weeks, an underground parking lot was designed and engineered to squeeze between the racetrack and perimeter wall of the marina. It would house all vehicles, golf carts, equipment, provisions, and staff accommodations necessary to operate and maintain a luxury yacht marina. The number of private parking spaces was increased substantially on the ground-level, high-exposure parking area that would sit on top of it. Additionally, the waterfront access road to the marina and yacht club would be widened into the channel to accommodate parking for more vehicles. The total number of spaces now came close to my estimate. The work began within days and without fanfare, environmental studies, or a municipal permit. Poof! Another seven figures of money ($3.5 million) were magically allocated from somewhere. Guaranteed, it did not originate from a bank requiring a comprehensive appraisal and a borrower's prequalification. Hundreds of laborers appeared on the job site, working under the direction of engineers and project directors who were already overextended. The site was transformed into a field of cranes, backhoes, excavators, and material supply and concrete lorries, all working in harmony and close proximity to one another. After viewing the speed with which large construction projects were completed in Abu Dhabi, I was not totally surprised that this underground parking lot was handed over in approximately four months.

The epic thirty-month Yas Island project includes, in addition to the marina and yacht club, a unique hotel that is one of the most complex ever constructed. It stands adjacent to, and was built concurrently with, the marina. The Yas Hotel, a five-star, five-hundred room architectural landmark, is cloaked in a grid-shell veil of 5,300 large LED panels that light up the evening sky with bursts of color. The hotel is one of the largest LED architectural projects in the world. Individually or synchronized, the Yas Marina Yacht Club and the Yas Hotel provide an unrivaled light show beginning at sunset.

Another complication arose. With construction of the marina well underway, a directive came down from the top to cantilever the hotel *over* the racetrack and *into* the marina. Egads! The marina basin could not be flooded until the construction of the part of the hotel that would be below the future high-water mark was completed, and the hotel's contractor figured a year would provide adequate time—for *him*. How about *me*? The already tight timetable for completion of the marina became tighter than tight. Project directors were left with no choice but to complete the interior of the enormous marina in a dry hole—no water—and complete the project within one year. Steel pilings were driven and concrete floating pontoons were assembled on a laser-graded sand bottom. Never in history had a marina of this scale been built "in the dry." And never in history had such an iconic yacht club and hotel been built adjacent to a marina. The three projects under simultaneous construction represented the pinnacle of innovation, technology, and architectural creativity.

Marina construction prior to flooding in 2009.
For scale, note the forty-foot container at right-rear.

Ticktock, Ticktock

It did not make sense. On one hand, the unwavering thirty-month deadline on Yas Island did not allow the luxury of scheduled or unscheduled time off. On the other, my colleagues and I were offered more time off from work than we would have been anywhere else and at any other time that I have seen in my adult life. How could such a momentous construction project be completed by forty-five thousand laborers when the skilled workers were absent 50 percent of the year? And the Yas Island project was merely *one* of the company's several ongoing multibillion dollar megadevelopment projects, with the others also employing thousands of laborers. From a 365-day year, deduct 104 days for weekends, 35 days for annual leave, approximately 15 for Muslim and Christian holidays, a few days for National Day and New Year's Day, and possibly another 4 for an unexpected passing of a member of one of the country's Royal Families. Before completing the math, factor in a month for Ramadan and another week for Eid al-Fitr, both time-honored periods within the Muslim faith. Whether a practicing Muslim or not, work hours are shortened for all employees during Islam's sacred days. Without considering sick leave or any other justified or unjustified leave, half of a work year has disappeared—gone. But the deadline remains.

At first, I felt guilty and continued to dedicate long hours to my responsibilities. But the system encourages an employee to take the thirty-five days of paid annual leave. Use them or lose them. My guilt decreased. The company offered attractive travel packages to preselected countries, difficult for an expat intent on seeking broad cultural exposure to ignore.

In the meantime, the clock continued to tick. The promise to deliver an iconic project on a specified date could not be altered. Saving face in the Emirati world carries more weight than the bottom line on a profit and loss worksheet. Financial statements are easily manipulated. It was vitally important to Abu Dhabi's Rulers to convey to the world that, in this case, the Yas Island development was their vision and their collection of dreams and daring creations that evolved into prominence for the emirate, the country, and the world. It is a vivid example of the expectations of Abu Dhabi's Rulers.

Just Do It

Back in high school physical education classes, I was relatively adept at performing jumping jacks, windmills, pull-ups, push-ups, and sit-ups. Yas Island colleagues taught me a new exercise—the shrug–palms up–eyeball roll—when I first questioned the magnitude of change orders, which were like none I could have ever imagined. When the Rulers decided to modify the shape of an island, replace a bridge with a tunnel, relocate a highway cloverleaf, or cantilever a hotel over a racetrack and into a marina, the exercise would begin. Seasoned project managers, engineers, contractors, and subcontractors all knew the routine: Raise shoulders to shrug level. Extend arms at the elbows with palms facing up. Roll eyeballs. This exercise was to be performed without an emotional outburst. Nonchalance is the key. When money is of little immediate consequence, momentous directional changes in a construction project frequently occurred at the snap of a finger.

The shrug–palms up–eyeball roll exercise froze project directors in their tracks when another decision from the top was announced a little over a year before the nonnegotiable completion date of the entire Yas Island project. A yet-to-be-built third bridge spanning the navigable waterway separating Yas Island from the mainland was to be replaced with a *tunnel*. The Rulers' decision was not a last-minute one; considering the scope of this complex project, it was a last-*second* decision. A 1.1-kilometer (0.66-mile) concrete tunnel consisting of six traffic lanes and a central cell for a future light-rail train would have to be completed within one year. Was it possible? A temporary earthen (sand) dam was built across the 150-meter-wide (490-foot) channel both upstream and downstream from the impending excavation. A fleet of large earth-moving equipment was transported to the site during the sixty days required to pump the water from between the dams and allow the excavation to dry out. Construction materials included twenty-seven thousand tons of steel and a hundred and sixty thousand cubic meters (192,000 cubic yards) of concrete, typically two of the more costly line items on a material cost breakdown in the Middle East. Once the tunnel was formed and the concrete poured and cured, the earthen dams were removed and the watertight tunnel was covered with a fraction of the previously excavated sand. The channel was dredged to a depth of seven meters (twenty-three feet) at low tide to accommodate the draft of a superyacht. The $22.2 million project, start to finish, was miraculously completed within a year—*and* four weeks prior to race day. It was a fingernail biter if there ever was one. Another seemingly impossible deadline had been met. I could not help but reflect on the inordinate length of time and cost invested to construct the new eastern span of the San Francisco–Oakland Bay Bridge back in California. That ongoing, $6.3 billion, taxpayer-financed project started in 2002 was originally scheduled to open in 2007. The ribbon cutting has now been moved forward to 2013—and that is optimistic. By comparison, half of the city of Abu Dhabi has been built in that eleven-year duration.

Jump First, Look Later

Many of us were aware of Dubai's often habitual lack of due diligence in addressing the sensitive coastal ecosystem during the rampant development of its waterfront in 2006–2008. The neighboring emirate's development companies more often than not worked against, not with, nature. Our engineers were cognizant of others' mistakes and paid lip service to avoiding the same to the degree possible while traveling supersonically. Many of the environmental obstacles had never been faced, let alone cleared. The repercussions were potentially irreversible if left unchecked. Growing pains were an unavoidable pitfall during the vault from a primitive existence to the twenty-first century over a mere forty years.

More than 70 percent of the UAE's drinking water originates from costly and energy-intensive desalination plants. The Undersecretary of the Ministry of Environment and Water was quoted in September 2011 as saying, "The UAE has around seventy water desalination plants, accounting for 14 percent of the world's total production of desalinated water." Removal of salt and other minerals from seawater to provide drinking water for human consumption and irrigation has allowed water-scarce countries to prosper. On the other hand, however, discharge from these plants has contributed to wiping out a significant percentage of the country's vast marine coral formations. According to a strategic analysis paper published in 2011 by the Global Food and Water Crises Research Program, through 2010 the UAE, Saudi Arabia, Bahrain, Qatar, Kuwait, and Oman together operate 1,483 desalination plants on the Arabian Gulf that desalinate approximately six million cubic meters of water daily, or 65 percent of the world's capacity. That is just shy of 8.5 *billion* 24-ounce bottles of drinking water per day. In the process, tons of brine-carrying chemicals are dumped back into the Gulf daily at the rate of one thousand–plus cubic meters per second, including an estimated twenty-four tons of chlorine, three hundred kilograms (660 pounds) of copper, and sixty-five tons of algae-harming antiscalants used to descale pipes. Back in California, green-blooded activists would be up in arms if they were made aware of this waste dump travesty. New desalination plants utilizing the latest technology from industrialized countries continue to be built to handle the massive population explosion in the Gulf countries coupled with the expected high standard of living. Concerned as I am over the adverse by-products of real estate development in the UAE, I was shocked to further discover that there were in excess of 14,500 desalination plants operating worldwide as of 2010, and the number continues to grow.

One of my first impressions of Abu Dhabi was of its lush presentation, beginning at the international airport. In Sheikh Zayed's words, "They say agriculture has no future [in the UAE], but with Allah's blessing and our determination, we have succeeded in transforming the desert into a green land." Thanks to Sheikh Zayed's guiding hand, 130 *million* trees, predominantly date palms, had been planted in Abu Dhabi as of 2007. The sides and center medians of multilane thoroughfares are lined with date palms and ghaf trees. Sculptured shrubbery and bountiful red, white, and purple petunias planted seasonally highlight the manicured lawn areas along major roadways. Roundabouts have artistic flower plantings and grandiose water features, and homeowners are urged to beautify their surroundings through government gifts of plants and trees. The emirate's luxuriant landscape requires an immense amount of irrigation water, recycled or potable. As of 2011, the UAE had emerged as the world's largest water consumer per capita, nearly 82 percent above the global individual average. The country's poor underground water resource, hot weather, scarce rainfall, rapid population growth, and lack of public awareness drive the high consumption. The demand for water is expected to nearly double by 2030, thereby requiring the construction of additional desalination plants. The challenge to provide the basic sustenance of life and, at the same time, protect and preserve the ecosystem continues in catch-22 perpetuity.

* *

Roadblocks, dead ends, screwups, *I-told-you-so*s, and profanity—no matter how unintentional—are humanly impossible to avoid when working at a speed approaching that of sound and setting production records. If a loose shoelace remains untied because of a time constraint, trouble lurks. When an oversight develops into a big uh-oh, the time to pout has passed.

A complex of mid- and high-rise residential buildings in the Al Raha Beach development across the channel from the Yas Marina racetrack was simultaneously under dust-raising construction. Individual units were being sold prior to their completion and prior to the racetrack's completion. A projected resident population of five thousand would eventually occupy the high-density neighborhood. On the opposite side of the channel, the racetrack was being built to accommodate nighttime racing. The prevailing wind reverses direction in the evening in Abu Dhabi and blows out of the Arabian

Gulf, across Yas Island, and toward the Al Raha Beach development. I anticipated that noise generated from the high-revving engines on the racetrack would be amplified by the water en route to the residential buildings located less than two kilometers (1.2-mile) from the source. Had the master planners of the project considered the high-decibel noise level that a Formula One race car generates? It is certainly not a line item on a builder's punch list. Would future residents find the intense noise annoying or a pleasing rhapsody? One way or the other, it would be loud. And yet, billions of dollars were being spent on construction of the combined developments. Deadlines took precedence over due diligence.

Out of curiosity, I Googled the Decibel Equivalent Table in 2008 during the pinnacle of construction activity. I was shocked to find that many of these future Al Raha Beach residents potentially faced hearing damage over time if they were to be on their balconies or leave a sliding door open with a prevailing evening wind during an F1 race. Earplugs are recommended to protect a person from hearing impairment when noise reaches 85 decibels, comparable to a Rolling Stones concert or an accelerating Harley Davidson motorcycle. The level approximates 120 decibels if one is standing next to a runway when a 747 jet takes off. Permanent hearing loss begins at 127 decibels without ear protection, and the threshold of pain is reached at 140 decibels. A 950-horsepower Formula One race car redlining at 18,000 revolutions per minute generates 147 decibels at trackside! This is unbelievably loud, louder than anything most people have ever heard in their lives. Unless already stone deaf, a resident might be utterly miserable without earplugs. I figured it would be a thoughtful gesture to include a couple of sets of earplugs in the new residents' welcome baskets.

Fast forward—I was a guest at an evening barbecue on an upper floor of a luxury villa in a mid-rise residential building that faced the now completed racetrack in the Al Raha Beach development. Junior varsity models of the F1 car, called GP2, were performing their practice laps in preparation for the weekend races. Sure enough, with a light breeze blowing out of the Arabian Gulf, it was difficult to carry on a civil conversation on the balcony overlooking the channel without shouting over the whine of the engines across the waterway, approximately 2.5 kilometers (1.5 miles) distant. For that matter, it would also have been difficult to converse if we were wearing earplugs. The host stood alone on his balcony flipping lamb burgers. He was the only human being visible on *any* balcony within the complex once the race cars commenced their practice laps. Thank goodness for television.

More and More
Ferrari World, the world's largest indoor theme park and another architectural and engineering marvel, was one more simultaneous Yas Island project whose exterior shell was completed by the company within the F1 race debut deadline. Its dimensions were staggering. The 200,000-square-meter (20-hectare or 49-acre) red roof was modeled after a side profile of the double-curved body shell of a Ferrari GT. It measures 7.8 football fields long with a 2.4-kilometer (1.4 mile) perimeter and features in the center the largest Ferrari prancing horse logo on a yellow shield ever created —65 meters (213 feet) across. The extraordinary structure is visible from space and an eyeful for passengers with window seats flying into or out of Abu Dhabi's international airport. An entry ticket to Ferrari World runs $45 to $102, depending upon the length of time one's attention can remain focused on Ferraris.

In 2006, Mubadala, an investment arm of the Abu Dhabi government, entered into negotiations with Ferrari to jointly promote Ferrari's F1 racing team, Team Ferrari—figuratively translated, *Scuderia Ferrari*. Formula One racing is Ferrari's only form of advertising, and winning races has historically been its favored means of marketing the treasured cars to the world. Results of the talks produced four benefactors: (1) Mubadala purchased 5 percent of Ferrari in early 2007; (2) Ferrari would receive massive promotional exposure ad infinitum on Abu Dhabi's Yas Island project; (3) Abu Dhabi would construct a motor sport racetrack to F1 specifications, as mentioned earlier, thereby providing the seventeenth international location on the Grand Prix circuit schedule; and (4) Abu Dhabi would further capitalize on its already exponentially expanding global media blitz.

Rounding out the Yas Island project were six additional luxury and boutique hotels, an eighteen-hole championship golf course and five-star clubhouse, freeways, cloverleafs, landscaped roadways, underground parking, cooling plants, and miles of complex underground infrastructure. This anthology of the momentous Yas Island construction project provides a picture of the prodigious scope of the development while keeping in mind that it was built, start to finish, in thirty months. Other momentous development projects were simultaneously popping out of the ground in both Abu Dhabi and Dubai, although few were as large, as comprehensive, or as costly as Yas. The $1.5 billion Burj Al Khalifa skyscraper in Dubai was an exception, taking top honors for being the tallest. I was an onlooker with big eyes. Focusing on one piece of the jigsaw puzzle was an overwhelming task in itself. Each element was complex, oftentimes a first, seemingly insurmountable, and, in two words, enthralling and mind-blowing.

Part Eight

Onward and Sideways
Vignettes

Pamela and I were immersed nonstop in cross-cultural encounters that would add many more chapters of ethnic insight to our chronicle of experiences. Of no surprise, that was fully our intent when we chose to relocate to the UAE. Acquaintances from Middle Eastern countries with whom I worked and socialized occasionally shared heart-wrenching stories of unimaginable hardship that they had experienced. The tales shocked me into questioning the value of Abu Dhabi's affluent lifestyle, inherited by nationals and Western expats, that insulated us from those less fortunate in lands so near.

A Palestinian couple hosted a party for its extended family and friends, and Pamela and I felt honored to be included. It was my first large social gathering since moving into the villa. Furniture and carpets had been cleared from the center of the hosts' enormous, marble-floored living room to provide room for dancing to songs played by a trio of Arabic musicians. Everyone from children through grandparents danced with jovial panache. A catered buffet of traditional Arabic food covered a long line of tables in the villa's beautifully landscaped backyard. While I was seated cross-legged on a traditional rug on the ground between two young Palestinian children, who were giggling and telling me a story, a low-flying military jet screamed by overhead. Both sisters jumped onto my lap, wrapped their little arms around me, buried their heads on my chest, and began to tremble uncontrollably. Their older brother told me that his sisters had watched Israeli jets bomb their house in Gaza the year before, killing their father's parents. Tears streamed down my cheeks as I held them tight.

Spice and Life

Other than the untimely disturbance caused by the military jet, many upbeat stories were shared that broadened cultural understanding and roused laughter. It was of no surprise to me that conversations among some of the ladies eventually drifted to the subject of shopping. I know from firsthand experience that it did not require more than one excursion to one of the many Iranian souks or opulent shopping malls before my wife experienced that sensation of arousal unique to the female species that only shopping can evoke. Souks, or traditional markets, employ an appropriately aggressive barter system in conducting financial transactions. The proprietors, predominantly Iranians, are particularly adept at the centuries-old practice. If the asking price of a hand-woven carpet is 2,200 dirham ($600), there is little reason for an accomplished barterer not to walk out of a shop with the carpet and only 1,450 dirham ($400) less in his or her pocket.

Pamela never reached the ranks of "accomplished," however. To the contrary, the astute souk shopkeeper relished the arrival of her familiar face. After trying on eighteen scarves and selecting one that looked similar to fourteen of the others, she would happily hand the prize scarf to the shopkeeper to be wrapped in a plastic grocery bag.

"Cost 40 dirham ($11), madam," he stated with a pained, sacrificial look.

Now, I had walked my wife through the intricacies of bartering on multiple occasions:

"Start with an offer of 60 percent of the asking price with a goal not to exceed 70 percent after the ensuing haggling. If that angle doesn't work, then walk. Chances are better than not that the shopkeeper will entice you back with a lower price—still higher than your original offer. Thank him and tell him his price is still too high."

Pamela eased into a Peace Corps mentality when it came to bartering. The shopkeeper had his timing down. He waited for the opportune moment to spring a suspicious-sounding story about his three-year-old daughter who tripped over a flowerpot and fractured a finger, and that moment coincided with his counter offer to Pamela's counter. My compassionate wife would break open her wallet and present the "father" with 100 percent of the original asking price, and he would offer Academy Award–winning gratitude while Pamela fought back tears. Both parties believed they were winners. The shopkeeper probably kicked himself for not saying that he had *two* daughters. But in the end, eleven dollars was not a bad price for an hand-embroidered silk scarf.

Dubai has established itself as a shopping mecca, and Abu Dhabi is rapidly catching up. One of several marble-encrusted, themed shopping malls on the Abu Dhabi side of Dubai is named after the well-traveled, fourteenth-century Arab explorer Ibn Battuta. The 265-store megamall is divided into six shopping zones, each with a theme related to Battuta's travels through Andalusia, Tunisia, Egypt, Persia, India, and China. My reluctance to spend more than thirty minutes shopping, exclusive of an exotic car showroom or hardware store, was outweighed by the mall's captivating cultural experience. That is precisely the premeditated reason that my wife believed she could corral me for over an hour. I knew better. It is not humanly possible for a woman to hit four shoe stores and five women's clothing stores in less than a week. I could easily cover the mall's territory blindfolded in less than forty-five minutes. The sales staff at chic Jimmy Choo-Choo, Yves Saint I Want, Coochi, Very Sassy, George R. Mighty, Pierre Cardboard, Louie Baton, and Betsey Johnson-

Evinrude probably plant magnets on their customers' wallets. When Pamela was not looking, I would line her purse with lead before entering the mall. I knew the magnet game, *insha'Allah*.

I refused to believe that I might be the sole red-blooded male who is bewildered when his wife has completed a marathon shopping escapade with nothing to show for it. Pamela calls it "tactile shopping." I have adopted less subtle names. On the rare occasion that "tactile" elevated to "purchase," a celebration was in order.

* *

Like many advanced societies, Abu Dhabi is proactive in its effort to reduce the use of plastic shopping bags. Careless trash dumping has killed many range camels that ingested plastic bags. The *National*, a local daily newspaper, initiated an awareness campaign and provided each of its thousands of subscribers with not one, but two, sisal bags—one large and one small. The large grocery stores were theoretically informed of the conservation crusade.

Soon thereafter, I was pleased to see sisal shopping bags in many grocery carts (*trolleys* in Brit-speak) pushed by Western expats in the Carrefour supermarket. My turn arrived at the checkout counter. The upbeat Filipina cashier handed my sisal bags to the uniformed Indian bag boy prior to scanning each grocery item and slid it along the counter to him. The bag boy proceeded to place the groceries into plastic bags. "*La! La!*" I exclaimed in Arabic. "No! No!" I pointed to the sisal bags lying beneath a full plastic bag, and he smiled and bobbed his head back and forth in apparent recognition of his oversight. I returned my attention to the cashier to pay for the groceries while the sisal bags were properly filled and placed in a shopping cart. When I reached my car in the underground parking lot and popped the trunk lid (*boot* in Brit), I had to laugh. The plastic bags full of groceries had been placed in the sisal bags.

Following my first solo grocery shopping spree, I experienced the maddening aftermath of failing to place grocery bags in the air-conditioned passenger compartment of the car, not the trunk where a person could heat soup. The twenty-minute drive back to the villa ended in a recitation of four-letter words the likes of which I had not uttered since watching my college team fumble the football in the final minute of a crucial game. Wilted lettuce, a melted Snickers bar, and a container of liquid coffee ice cream rank high on life's register of disappointments.

In mid-2008, three large trash recycling bins were placed in a central location in our villa compound. The containers were colored traffic-yellow and unmarked. As such, they merely served as another receptacle in which to toss unseparated refuse comprising paper, glass, aluminum, wet garbage, and landscape clippings. It was only after a conscientious Western expat had labeled the bins with a wide-tipped, permanent marker pen that other residents believed the confusion had been properly addressed. Two stumbling blocks were overlooked: first, the domestic help, or housekeeper(s), in each villa are responsible for the disposal of the villa's garbage, and Western expats, the legal sponsors of the domestic staff, had not provided them the necessary education and guidance to employ this new phenomenon called *recycling*. And second, a dump is a dump in the minds of the those from the lesser-developed world. Who cares whether an aluminum can is buried in the sand with landscape clippings? Out of sight is out of sight. The learning curve for trash recycling in our villa complex did not significantly deviate from a horizontal line. Over 90 percent of the emirate's collected solid waste ended up in a landfill prior to 2010.

The neighborhood grocery store is called a food stuffs. When a food stuffs' clerk, who doesn't speak or understand English but fakes his comprehension of it, is asked where a grocery item is located, he will generally escort—a nice touch—the lost soul to the general location of the "needful" and ask in an illogical blend of languages how many "pieces" are desired. The pidgin-English-speaking clerk behind the fish and meat counter expects *pieces* to be translated into kilos. That's all well and fine for every inhabitant on the planet exclusive of most all Americans who have not learned the metric system or did not major in math. My wife minored. She would hold her hands up over the counter and cup them to indicate the portion of pieces she wanted. It always worked. It also generated polite chuckles from the math majors. Once back in our villa and seated at the dinner table, Pamela would get her revenge by asking straight-faced how many pieces of needful I would like. I would cup my hands.

Spices have been used for centuries for food additives—flavoring and coloring—perfume, and cosmetics. Magicians have long incorporated spices in their hocus-pocus acts and morticians in embalming. The Middle East has been integral in the trade of spices, often transported by camel caravans across the deserts, since at least 2,000 BC. Spices have been, and presently are, an integral ingredient in the preparation of Middle Eastern food, much of which has Indian influence. India, a not-too-distant neighbor of the UAE, produces more spices than any other country in the world. Spices are also one of my wife's weaknesses. I thank Allah that diamonds are not another.

Following her earlier trips to Dubai and Abu Dhabi, Pamela would mention to me how the groups of journalists with whom she was traveling had visited Dubai's gold souk and, tempted by glitter and competitive prices, would load their bags with trinkets of gold—or bling. She, on the other hand, hung out in Dubai's open-air spice souk with small shops tucked along each side of a narrow walkway featuring gunnysacks and crude wooden barrels filled to the top with spices of every hue and fragrance. Instead of earrings and bracelets, she returned to California with clothes permeated with the aroma of cloves, cinnamon, and cumin because of the bags of spices packed in her luggage.

She enjoys the kitchen (*galley* in boat-speak) and wasted no time taking advantage of her time in the UAE to learn more about spices and cooking in the local style. As I happily tasted her new dishes, she would relate the finer points that she had learned: that nutmeg traded during the Middle Ages was highly esteemed and sold for high prices as it was believed to ward off infectious disease; that the most commonly used early spices were black pepper, cinnamon, cumin, nutmeg, ginger, and cloves; and that Indian cooking generally incorporates a blend of no less than six flavorful spices in dishes, a combination known by its English name, curry. They were used not only for flavor but to balance food's yin and yang. She lost me back at "infectious disease."

Daughter Stephanie enchanted with spices in spice souk

Her passion to learn as much as possible about Arabic cooking and its influences was aided by her broadening photojournalistic reach into mainstream magazines. She accepted a unique offer to cover the ten-day Gourmet Abu Dhabi, a gastronomical festival. She was delighted to mingle with master chefs and pâtissiers from internationally acclaimed restaurants and sporting Michelin Stars, taste her way through food reviews, and partake in the decadent events at several locations in the city, including the Emirates Palace and Shangri-La. As her spouse, I was more than readily available to assist in the tasting at several of the events that permitted a chaperone or hungry quasi-connoisseur.

The editor of a local magazine realized she had found someone who truly knew and liked food. Pamela was invited to join in a new undertaking—helping to coordinate the inaugural cooking competition for the Annual Date Festival in Al Liwa, a desert oasis two hours by car east of the city of Abu Dhabi. Believing she would be among people who loved food and from whom she could learn, she embraced the opportunity with Wild West enthusiasm. Her responsibility, it seemed, was to organize the competition. She established guidelines and rules for the festival and contacted chefs from the major hotels in Abu Dhabi to see who could and would participate in the white-tablecloth extravaganza. Each chef and his staff were required to prepare and present a three-course meal that, of course, incorporated dates. Dates are significant in a sizable part of the history and culture of the Arabian people. Desert nomads often relied on a steady diet of dates and everything camel for months on end. It is said that a person can survive exclusively on dates, rich in vitamins A and B, dietary fiber, and camel milk, which, in turn, is high in potassium, iron, and vitamin C. Today, the UAE is the largest exporter of dates and date derivatives in the world.

Pamela spent the next three weeks on the phone and e-mail planning menus, scheduling kitchen times for the two-day event, making sure that entry paperwork was returned, and checking the level of commitment from participants. It would not be appropriate to disappoint members of the Royal Family planning to attend the well-publicized, prize-giving finale. Chefs are, by definition, experts on producing delightful and delectable food and are not necessarily fettered by the concerns of day-to-day communication. During the final week of preparations, when her stress level was noticeably elevated, I overheard her mumble something about herding cats. The chefs who decided to participate were lured by the lucrative prizes but perhaps more by the publicity they would receive—always good for business and headlines on a resume. The talented and hard-working group was accustomed to the instantaneous and momentous demands of their jobs. They leaned into the traces, didn't blink an eye, and created menus for dishes that included some of the eighty-plus varieties of locally grown dates.

The event was not without a last-minute roller coaster ride of issues. Two chefs, who apparently had just looked up from their kitchen duties to find the map to the Al Liwa oasis, decided on the day preceding the event that it was too far to travel. No cajoling would change their minds. But the 42°C (107°F) midday desert temperature did not discourage the attendance of twelve thousand guests and participants even though the immense, air-conditioned tents simply could not keep up with demand. Chefs were sweating under their toques and pressed whites as they cheerily produced their inventive menus on and in new, top-of-the-line European cookers provided by the festival's sponsors. When one of the judges did not show up, no problem—Pamela happily filled the slot. She was in her culinary element and was rewarded with an opportunity to taste the results of the chefs' hard work and planning. The chefs and their staffs excelled. Pamela was happy to receive invitations to visit her newfound chef friends in their hotels' kitchens and continue the association.

For date aficionados, some of the creative menu items included foie gras terrine with balsamic dates, quenelle of dates, sauces with dates, roasted lamb with pistachio crust and date au jus, kebab with date flavors, chicken stuffed with dates, date cakes and puddings with camel milk cream topping, date macaroon, and sponge cake with date mousse. I fully expected that our diet in the ensuing weeks would consist of date salad, date pie, date syrup, date stuffing, date ice cream, plain dates, marinated dates, and pickled dates, all washed down with a date cooler. I entertained going on a food strike.

Emirati hospitality—tea and dates served with a smile

Survival of the Fittest

Air conditioners and water heaters in our villa were located above the ceiling in each of the six bathrooms. The bathroom ceilings were composed of large, lightweight tin tiles that snap into and out of an aluminum framework, providing access to the mechanical units. Our villa contained six air conditioners and six water heaters, all electric-powered in this land of plentiful natural gas. (Natural gas is used to generate electrical power in the UAE.)

Shortly after we moved into our sparkling-clean villa, water began to drip incessantly from a ceiling tile in the center of one of the bathrooms whenever the AC was on, which was two-thirds of the year. Inquisitively, I pried out a ceiling tile and observed that the condensate line connection on the bottom of the AC unit was dripping. It appeared to be an easy fix. I notified the leasing company's maintenance department of the leak.

Two Indian repairmen arrived within two hours without a single tool or a ladder. Barefoot, one of them hopped from the edge of the tub onto the granite vanity top cantilevered out from the wall to view the source of the leak. Using body language in lieu of speaking Urdu, I discreetly suggested to him that his body weight might jeopardize the integrity of the countertop attached to the wall. The acrobat instructed his sidekick to bend over and grab the lip of the toilet bowl in order that he may place one foot on his back to lessen the strain on the vanity and better reach the condensate line. I'm thinking, *Ladder*. He doesn't know "ladder." With more animation, I pointed out that the countertop is not intended to function as a trampoline. Aha! He got it! A veteran charades player.

The talented duo returned an hour later with a length of weathered wood that had been pried off a pallet. They wedged the board under the edge of the countertop at an angle because it was too long to be plumb. The ambidextrous Indian who had earlier stooped over the toilet bowl placed a bare foot against the base of the angled board to prevent it from scooting out from under the countertop under half the weight of the highly skilled Indian condensate-line repairman. As a precautionary measure, he again grabbed the lip of the toilet bowl while bending over from the waist, imitating a partly opened pocket knife, to serve as a step stool. This guy was *good*. The acrobat tweaked the PVC pipe with a leftover length of rusty baling wire, found hanging conveniently from a metal duct above the ceiling, and properly angled the drain line as per the manufacturer's installation instructions. It was a first-class repair utilizing critical thinking from the lesser-developed world. The maintenance department might still be working on the repair today if its staff had been employed by a Western municipal utility district that adhered to safety standards and required liability insurance.

Shoveling snow off a driveway is one thing; sweeping and mopping drifting sand off marble flooring is entirely another. Shortly after moving into the villa, I was informed by Frederic and Jolanda, two Belgian work colleagues, that it was impossible to keep the fine desert sand dust from migrating inside. They were correct. With all doors and windows closed, fine sand particles still magically appeared like meat bees and ants at a picnic. Polished marble-floored hallways become ideal shuffleboard lanes for competitive barefoot or sandal skidding. My British neighbors were fairly laid-back about it: "We haven't bean keen on sand whilst we've bean 'ere with other mates, but we've learnt how to lyve with it."

Our villa's bathrooms, kitchen, and utility room were delineated from connecting rooms or hallways by a raised marble threshold in order to retain the generous amount of water used in mopping the floors. A floor drain was randomly located in each room to collect the dust-laden water that was squeegeed into it by the housekeeper, and the damp floors dried within minutes. The cleaning ritual was repeated every few days.

Sudden squalls, or *shamals*, that frequently whipped up and down the coast with no apparent rhyme or reason compounded the sandy nuisance. They often brought clouds of sand that reduced visibility to a level similar to that in a snow blizzard. Outdoor workers wrapped their traditional head scarves around their heads and necks for protection, leaving only a slit for their eyes. Sand drifts accumulated on the front windshields of cars, oftentimes overcoming the wipers' ability to remove the nuisance. Unfortunately, sand does not melt like snow. One shamal was all that was needed for me to remember to close the vehicle compartment's outside air intake during a sandstorm to avoid a sand-dust tsunami *inside* the car. Once the wind subsided, workmen wielding square-tipped shovels and brooms diligently removed the sand drifts from roadways.

The migrant labor force is used in many situations where heavy equipment would be immensely more efficient to complete the task. Because of my construction background, the reasoning did not compute. I perceived it to be a waste of manpower. The Abu Dhabi government is certainly financially capable of purchasing a front-end loader or six to remove sand from roadways and a backhoe to dig a ditch. A thousand-strong workforce cost more over time than a piece of heavy equipment. Even so, the work performed by the unskilled labor force, despite requiring significantly more time, is impeccable. All parties are winners. Nationals kept their contract workforce employed, residents appreciated the finished product, and the government was not out the cost of a front-end loader.

I found that underground parking lots are next to imperative in Abu Dhabi to minimize a building's footprint on valuable sand and to provide shelter from the sun's intense rays. To an expat who had not yet acclimated to the higher temperatures, the underground lots felt like the inside of a kitchen oven (*cooker* in Brit-speak) on a low setting. Above-ground parking areas are, more often than not these days, provided with shade covers for protection. It was not solely my concern that the plastic steering wheels in our cars might melt while parked unprotected during the late spring, summer, and early fall months.

Thankfully, the onshore sea breeze begins to cool the island in October. Daytime temps become a comfortable 24–30°C (75–85°F), evening temps occasionally drop to a chilly 19°C (66°F), and the electric bill reflects the plunge, *insha'Allah*. The rainy season is fleeting. The average annual rainfall is 50–125 millimeters (2–5 inches), falling predominantly in February and March. One day of rain totaling 13 millimeters (about half an inch) leaves the ground and streets looking like a monsoon had struck. Abu Dhabi is perfectly flat. The sand does not leach as I had expected in a desert, and the underground storm-drain pipes are often restricted by sand accumulated over the previous eleven-plus months. Many residents hold firm the belief that a couple of days of puddles far outweigh the comparative devastation following a "major storm"—like 50 millimeters (2 inches)—that most of the rest of the world get. The biggest inconvenience is a dirty Mercedes.

I developed a habit of swimming most every afternoon after work in the sheltered waters off the beach that bordered our compound of villas. Only one swim was required to convince me of the necessity of leaving sandals at the water's edge to avoid getting third-degree burns while walking to and from the water on the scalding-hot sand. The accessories were as imperative as a swimsuit—maybe more so. At first, I thought I was losing it when I discovered that my swimsuit was dry prior to completing the three-minute walk back to the villa. One picture remains vivid: I caught sight of two Brits playing tennis at high noon on a green-surfaced asphalt court in 43°C (109°F) temperature, clothed in spiffy white Tommy Bahama tennis shorts and tennies—no shirts. Nowhere was a bottle of water, visor cap, or bottle of anti-insanity pills to be seen. These blokes were undoubtedly the bloody mad dogs and Englishmen that Joe Crocker pictured when composing his 1970 album. I was relieved to see them alive that evening, although pan-fried, half-baked, and dehydrated, with blood-shot eyes.

Why Make It Simple When Complexity Works Just Fine?

Every country has its unique set of criteria that make up its established officialdom. A resident of his homeland has more than likely developed a familiarity with his country's bureaucratic formalities and has learned to expect and even accept them. A nonresident, or expat, on the other hand, is typically less familiar with the rules, requirements, and expectations necessary to wade through the red tape specific to a foreign country. More to the point, Western impatience with time-consuming, bang-your-head-against-a-wall type of bureaucracy is unavoidable on much of the Arabian Peninsula. Asians and Africans have a grip on it, and locals know how to bypass it. Westerners have higher blood pressure.

A different means of functioning, or modus operandi, as defined by Western standards, prevails among a majority of UAE expats from the lesser-developed countries. It elicits as much humor as frustration. Although superb visionaries, even many educated nationals have an intellectual composition that is oftentimes less digital and more analog even though they rely on established methods of Western analytical thinking. The UAE would take a step backward in its quantum leap onto the global stage without its white-collar workforce composed of Western-educated critical thinkers.

The challenge of locating a business in Abu Dhabi (or Dubai) can require guidance from a deity. A street may be called something entirely different from the name identified on a street sign. A street map, if you can find one, is a ticket to purgatory. But *most* disconcerting is the absence of street address numbers. Abu Dhabi is a city whose population approaches 800,000 and whose street number population is zero. The post office, simply called the post, consequently does not provide door-to-door mail delivery. Incoming personal mail is instead delivered to a numbered post box, where it is picked up by an employee's company representative and distributed to employees internally. Conversely, outgoing mail is collected and transported to the post by the employer. An individual *may* elect to pay for a personal post box; however, post locations on the island are few and far between.

Abu Dhabi nationals do not *need* addresses. They know buildings by their names and businesses by their owners. "That business is in the Soraya building," an Emirati might say. *And where is the Soraya building?* "Next to the Maloof building." *And where is …?* This futile question-and-answer conversation is par for the course.

Pamela and I had one such protracted reconnaissance venture on our first excursion downtown. After crossing the Mussafah Bridge and driving the length of the island, we lucked out and arrived in the general neighborhood of our destination. We double- or triple-parked (not uncommon at that time) our car and entered the nearest conveniently located building to seek the kind assistance of an employee for direction. Many businesses are predominantly manned by the semi-*trained*, not semi-educated, working-class folks who reside downtown in the many high-rise residential buildings. They either walk or take taxis to work and so do not view direction from the perspective of a car's driver. It can be difficult to get into their mind-set. They generally do not understand what we ask them, and we do not understand why they do not understand. The cross-cultural confusion can be hilarious or frustrating. Take your pick. I recommend the former.

With unwavering determination and more luck, we stumbled across the mystery location of the business we had begun seeking more than an hour earlier. We entered the front door only to be told, in a mixture of Urdu or Hindi-broken English, that the *specific* location is two doors farther down the sidewalk and upstairs. Following keen directions, we entered a stark lobby with somewhat up-to-date signage identifying a floor or business and rode an elevator, called a lift, capable of holding six thin adults to Floor 1—*two* floors above the lobby or ground level. Exiting into a hallway with no signage, we entered the first door we came to and ... we arrived! But it was prayer time. Employees were understandably nowhere to be found. Business had come to a temporary halt. Once up and rolling again twenty minutes later, an ebullient sign language–speaking clerk asked how she could be of service. The heck if I could recall. That was two hours ago.

An event representing a futile attempt at efficiency occurred in mid-2009 on the UAE-Saudi border. The Kingdom of Saudi Arabia (KSA) set up a roadblock to perform eye scans on and fingerprint all truck drivers entering the kingdom, purportedly to control the transport of black-market Gucci, Armani, and Rolex goods. To set the scene, a logjam of lorries was stretched over thirty-two kilometers (nineteen miles). The haulers from Qatar, Bahrain, Oman, and the UAE that traverse Saudi to deliver goods to Jordan, Lebanon, and Syria were parked in a no-man's land for days in 45°C (113°F) temps without food, water, or basic hygienic facilities. Engines had to remain running to operate the air conditioners so that the drivers wouldn't dehydrate. Without a supply of diesel to keep the refrigerated lorries that were carrying perishable goods cold for multiple days, millions of kilos of products were spoiled (*spoilt* in Oxford-speak). What created the traffic snarl? The Saudi security force had not been trained to operate the eye-scan and fingerprint equipment.

Rules of Engagement
My first exposure to driving in the United Arab Emirates occurred one minute after exiting the Dubai International Airport terminal in 2007. The chauffeur drove like a Bangkok taxi driver. He almost succeeded in frightening us into returning to the terminal and flying back to the place we had departed twenty-one hours earlier. He clearly demonstrated that aggressive driving skills were the rule of the road. He was a model aggressor.

I soon recognized, or rationalized, that there was somewhat of a logical reason why the accident rate on UAE highways is inordinately high and survival requires keen, defensive driving skills. The first paved roadways in Abu Dhabi were not constructed until approximately 1970 and, once completed, were shared by camels, Land Rovers, and thirty Mercedes. Driver's licenses were not issued for many years because there was no government oversight. In the developed world, meanwhile, millions of vehicles driven by licensed drivers had been plying paved roads since before the First World War. Emiratis suffer a ninety-year disadvantage in their continuing struggle to become proficient drivers. While college friends in the States were driving Dodge Chargers or Pontiac GTOs or Corvette Stingrays in 1970, most Emiratis were driving four-legged animals or walking. Only two generations have passed since that time.

During my three-year residency in Abu Dhabi, I never observed or heard of a traffic officer pulling over a motorist on the highways for any reason, lorries being the exception.

A contingent of policemen would occasionally set up a checkpoint where they would flag lorries to the side of the highway and inspect them to make sure that there was a tolerable amount of rubber left on the tires. The policemen handled the checkpoints, provided a protective shield for dignitaries, and responded to reported vehicle accidents, but they did not issue citations for speeding, spewing a black exhaust cloud, or littering. An expired registration, burned-out headlamp, excessive load of cargo (or workmen), and a lengthy list of other offenses that a California highway patrolman would find enticing were also disregarded. Modern technology has replaced the human in detecting speeding infractions. Stealthy radar machines are permanently located throughout the emirate (and Dubai) to record drivers who exceed the allowable twenty kilometers (12 miles per hour) over the posted speed limit. I never figured out how the taxi drivers know which machines operate and which do not. Maybe they unplug them or spray paint the camera lenses. If a driver is electronically caught exceeding the allowable speed limit, he or she is notified of the infraction via a text message on his or her mobile.

Abu Dhabi has followed the lead of other developed nations in citing drivers caught talking on a mobile phone while holding it to the ear. Lo and behold, I was nailed. I received two text messages from an attentive camera monitor stating that I was a bad boy. One message was in Arabic, the other in English, and they provided an e-mail address for the convenience of paying the 220-dirham ($60) citation with a credit card.

Traffic citations are tracked at the Department of Motor Vehicles, and all citations must be paid prior to reissuance of a vehicle's annual registration. My day arrived. Sure enough, the clerk handed me a picture of the rear license plate on my Toyota SUV that had been snapped eight months earlier along with a bill for 600 dirham ($164). It was futile to request details of the citation. It was printed in Arabic, and the kind, shaylah-covered desk clerk conveniently spoke only Arabic. *Patience. Grin and pay it.*

Roadways become dangerously slippery from sand dust that accumulates between the long absences of rain. Many drivers do not have a clue how to drive with caution under those conditions. I had just driven across the Maqta Bridge onto Abu Dhabi island in rush-hour traffic during a light rain. Traffic remained congested while moving at 70 kilometers per hour (42 miles per hour) as the road bore into a gentle turn to the right. A Toyota Land Cruiser in the lane to my right continued to drive straight and T-boned the midsize Tata van immediately in front of me. Vehicle accident protocol requires that the drivers of all vehicles involved in an accident stop in their tracks, call 999, and wait for a traffic officer to arrive, who makes a determination on the spot of who was at fault and who was not. Paperwork is handed to the drivers to either submit to their auto insurance carriers or, if at fault, to the Department of Motor Vehicles. The department may revoke a driver's license, impound the vehicle, issue a jail sentence, or all of the above, particularly for a laborer without a benefactor.

Traffic came to a halt, it was raining, and ten minutes passed before a traffic officer managed to squeeze through the congestion. The driver of the Land Cruiser was a young Emirati male who may have been fourteen years old at most. The driver of the van was an Iranian shopkeeper and was in a state of panic. Although the young national was clearly at fault, his Land Cruiser's license plate had three digits, meaning he was well connected. The traffic officer politely instructed the underage driver to drive away, most likely to safeguard his own job security. I figured the expat laborer would be declared at fault. I hopped out of my car into the rain and explained to the officer that I had observed the accident and insisted that the van's driver was obviously not at fault. I was well aware that I had stuck my expat neck out by questioning an Emirati police officer in the Emirati world, but I apparently prevailed. The officer drove away without having issued documentation to either driver. The shopkeeper, who spoke Farsi and probably minimal Arabic, was ecstatic that he would not lose his driver's license, spend time in jail, or possibly have his work visa canceled and therefore get deported. He hustled back to his van, opened the rear doors (the passenger-side doors had been crushed in the accident), grabbed a long, rolled-up rug, hefted it onto his shoulder, and insisted that I accept it as a token of his appreciation. There was no way I would accept a gift for standing my ethical ground. With eyes watering, he placed a hand over his heart. "You take. You take," he pleaded. By this time in my residency, I had learnt (darned Brit lingo) that if I refused, I would be considered aloof or unappreciative, even rude. I nodded and said, "*Shukran*" (*SHOE-kron*). Thank you.

Once back at the villa, I shared the story with Pamela. She asked where the rug was since I had neglected to retrieve it from the car. When I returned with the roll, we unrolled it and were shocked to find that it was an expensive Kashmir silk rug. The event was another example of the balancing act with life's precious freedoms. It was also a vivid example of the many unqualified drivers on UAE roads.

The road sign that reads "Watch for Road Surprises" is an eye-catcher. Is one to suspect that something might pop out from behind a palm tree while speeding down the freeway? Is the creator of this sign aware that many Western expat drivers have won a stuffed bear at the shooting gallery at a county fair for assassinating a surprise? *Surprises* here pertains to a wayward camel or freeway jaywalker.

Back in the States, I have no recollection of batting an eyelash while motoring past a rural field containing a herd of cattle or horses or even of subconscious alarm over a possible fender-bender or serious injury accident with one of the four-legged animals because fencing prevents the animals from wandering onto a roadway. In the desert, camels replace cattle and horses, and fencing had been installed along most, but not all, of the primary roadways in the UAE prior to my relocation to Abu Dhabi. Secondary roads are hit-and-miss, pun intended. The aftermath of a vehicle collision with a camel was a terrifying sight. Unlike a 700-kilo (1,500-pound) ground-hugging cow, an equally heavy dromedary camel stands approximately 1.8 meters (6 feet) at the shoulder, well above the bonnet (*hood* in Webster's) height of a passenger vehicle. When struck by a vehicle traveling at 100 kilometers per hour (60 miles per hour), a camel's body mass is capable of shearing off everything in its path above the height of the bonnet. A "road surprise" sign was not to be ignored.

Most trucks and buses pull over to the right shoulder of a roadway within sight or earshot of a mosque at the beginning of each of the five daily calls to prayer, but there is a 50 percent chance that a mosque is located on the opposite side of the roadway. If the driver and his occupant(s), predominantly Muslims from Iran, Pakistan, or Afghanistan, choose to perform their prayer obligations in a mosque that falls into this half rather than being adjacent to their vehicles, they also become road surprises.

If citations for traffic violations were issued by the policemen in Abu Dhabi and Dubai as scrupulously as they are in the States, the queue of cited violators would wrap twice around the block at the emirates' Department of Motor Vehicles. A driver's immersion certificate, my fictitious wallpaper diploma, is *not* a prerequisite to receive a UAE driver's license. But it should be. Likewise, basic driving coursework is not a requirement. But it should be. In my eccentric dreams, I suggested to the Driver Education Department, a subdepartment of the Department of Higher Complexity, or possibly the Department of Redundancy Department, that the following classes become mandatory:

Course – Basic UAE Freeway Driving 1A
Offered – 7 days/week, 24 hours/day
Minimum age – Proof not required
Duration of course – 1 hour
Syllabus:

(1) Drive like a lunatic.
(2) Posted speed limit is *not* to be observed. Driving at 40 km/h (24 mph) over the posted speed limit may, or may not, merit a snapshot from a radar camera.
(3) Do *not* leave more than two meters (a little over six feet) between bumpers while drafting.

(4) The trailing, or drafting, vehicle may blink high beams relentlessly regardless of the time of day to irritate or terrify the driver of the leading vehicle.

(5) Do *not* hesitate to pass a very fast-moving vehicle with a faster-moving vehicle on the left shoulder.

(6) It is frowned upon to clip side-view mirrors while overtaking or being overtaken.

(7) Pedestrians have no rights.

Course – Basic UAE Truck and Bus Driving 1A
Offered – During rush hour
Minimum age – Proof not required
Duration of course – 2 hours or until first accident
Ethnicity – Iranian, Afghan, Pakistani, Indian
Syllabus:

(1) Drive like a lunatic.

(2) Traditional Arabic beads may be hung from mud flaps and sun visors.

(3) Truck or bus may spew the maximum amount of black carbon residue from its exhaust pipe to prevent the UAE from becoming a carbon-neutral country.

(4) Overloaded labor buses may make every effort to ride up on two wheels when cornering.

(5) What are pedestrians?

Driver's Immersion Certificate
The fictitious course is an assimilation primer covering the country's rules of the road. All UAE expatriates must possess a valid driver's immersion certificate prior to receipt of a residency visa from the Immigration and Visa Department and prior to application for a UAE driver's license.

Offered – Beginning the day following entry into UAE
Minimum age – Proof not required
Duration of course – Length of residency in the UAE
Syllabus:

(1) Locals tint all windows of their vehicles so an observer cannot see an underage driver.

(2) Locals honk the horns of their Bentleys in front of laundry shops, food stuffs, and pizza parlors to alert a shopkeeper to deliver product ordered via mobile to their waiting vehicles.

(3) Locals do not alter their driving habits during blinding sandstorms and the brief periods of rain when roadway surfaces become grease.

(4) Locals believe an accelerator pedal is intended to be depressed to the floorboard.

(5) Locals ignore radar cameras because the cost of a speeding citation is inconsequential.

(6) Locals own all the high-testosterone vehicles on Abu Dhabi roadways.

(7) Locals rule the road. Pedestrians rule nothing.

Part Nine

Checkered Flag

The Yas Marina and the exterior shell of the Yas Marina Yacht Club were completed, without divine intervention, one month prior to the Formula One Grand Prix. Senior project directors had avoided the mythical one-way ticket to the Empty Quarter. I was ecstatic that the marina team had performed flawlessly in spite of the unforeseen roadblocks. The captains of several of the luxury yachts that would soon adorn the marina offered their accolades. It was now a matter of performance. Would everything within the marina operate as planned? Would the intensive training of the marina's dockhands demonstrate the six-star customer service that had been called for in no uncertain terms by the Sheikh back at Pearls & Caviar? The entire marina team was metaphorically in the championship game of the World Cup and expected to prevail.

The logistics designed to welcome incoming luxury yachts required multilingual organization. Specific berths had been reserved in advance by VIPs and VVIPs based upon the lengths of their vessels and a preferential location to view the race from the tiered decks on their yachts. The operators of several smaller (a matter of perspective) yachts conveniently forgot how to converse in English in an ill-fated attempt to squeeze into a premier trackside berth. The sky buzzed with private and government helicopters dropping off yacht owners and their high-profile guests. The level of security was unrivaled.

Sometimes you gotta do what you gotta do. Think outside the box, and quickly. One of the spectacular megayachts to arrive was too long to fit in the marina and had to be secured to the quay wall in the channel immediately outside the entrance. The location offers an unobstructed view of one of most exciting sections of the racetrack, incorporating four ninety-degree turns. In order to provide a comparable view for guests on other long yachts on the quay wall, the captain agreed to secure his mistress (the yacht) to shore Mediterranean-style (stern in, bow out). The combination of a 91-meter (297-foot) vessel and a comparatively narrow channel left little choice but to have the dock lines on her bow span the remaining short distance across the channel and be secured to an immoveable object on land. Like what? It's a desert. The cool, calm, and collected marina staff arranged for two large bulldozers to be transported promptly to the opposite side of the channel and attached each of the two bow dock lines to a bulldozer, which pulled the lines taut, safely securing the nine-figure floating palace. The marina staff was certainly not going to raise the issue that the channel was now impassable to other large yachts. The megayacht was owned by a Ruler, as was the marina and everything else within sight.

Etihad A340 fly-by, Abu Dhabi's national airline
sporting its Formula One sponsorship logo

The Yas Hotel cantilevered over the Formula One racetrack
and into the marina. Note the F1 car on the track.

Unobstructed trackside viewing from the decks of luxury yachts

Big boys' toys

5,300 LED panels on the Yas Hotel displayed the checkered flag
as the winning Formula One race car crossed the finish line.

Race day arrived. A fleet of over one hundred new buses
had been imported from Germany specifically for this event to
transport enthusiasts to and from the track. Hundreds of young
Emirati volunteers, each wearing a warm ambassadorial smile, were
strategically located and available to answer questions and provide
direction. The grandstands were packed with forty-one thousand
race fans. A new Etihad wide-body Airbus 340 jet, with the official
F1 logo painted on its fuselage and four engines and racing's famous
checkered flag painted on its tail, performed a low fly-by over the
racetrack. Pride filled the hearts of those present as Abu Dhabi's
national airline displayed its noble sponsorship. Earplugs were
inserted, and the starting flag dropped to signify the start of the
race that represented the culmination of work performed by a city
of migrant laborers and thousands of gifted international expats and
nationals. The timely completion of the never-before-attempted,
off-the-chart projects was what I construed to be a construction

miracle. We had met the challenge and achieved what I and others had believed to be unachievable. The choreography required to complete one of the largest construction projects undertaken in recent centuries was extraordinary.

Worldwide TV viewership statistics are considered practically unverifiable. Nevertheless, Abu Dhabi's print media reported that the televised Grand Prix was viewed globally by an estimated 600 million race fans, the third-highest number of TV viewers in sports history behind the World Cup and the Summer Olympic Games. UAE Royals, along with heads of state, *Fortune 500* CEOs, film and rock stars, hardcore race fans, those who were along for the ride, and want-to-be-seeners enjoyed ringside seats for the race from the decks of $25–$150 million superyachts at Yas Marina. Many of the world's largest private luxury yachts were in attendance. It was Abu Dhabi's Camelot moment—and mine. The emirate's economy reaped an estimated half-billion dollars in total revenue attributable to Formula One week.

* *

Much of the additional master-planned development on Yas Island remains incomplete today, a victim of the global economic downturn. Many billions of dollars were nevertheless spent on phase one of four planned phases prior to this writing. A Warner Bros. theme park, a regional supermall, five additional marinas, sports and entertainment complexes, and residential neighborhoods may be included in future phases. The total development was valued at $40 billion in 2007, with a completion date of 2020 and a projected resident population of a 110,000—all dictated by the economy. In the Western world, the numbers are profound. But in Abu Dhabi, they represent easily achievable goals. Whenever the completion date arrives, Yas Island is expected to be patronized by some of the most affluent people in the world. Mubadala purchased the lion's share of the completed phase one in February 2010 for an estimated $9.1 billion from the predominantly government-owned development company that built it, my former employer. "Government-owned" and "non-direct government owned" are used interchangeably, their meanings a matter of interpretation. It is tantamount to shifting money from one pocket to the other.

Part Ten

"The sky's falling! The sky's falling!"

—*Chicken Little*, Disney, 1943

"Now this is not the end. It is not even the beginning of the end. But it is, perhaps, the end of the beginning."

—Sir Winston Churchill, 1942

Who's Holding the Old Maid?

Economic fundamentals are relatively boilerplate. Intuition drives a financial investment. The investor, regardless of whether it is an individual, company, or market fund, rides a groundswell of confidence to, hopefully, derive a profit. Risk is leveraged to purchase an asset perceived to be undervalued. Prices oftentimes reach illogical levels. When the global economy turned about the time that Lehman Brothers collapsed in September 2008, confidence and euphoria turned to fear. Investors rushed to disengage from financial commitments. Prices plunged. *Bang*—the bubble popped. Both creditors and debtors were uncertain of who held the Old Maid. She was one indebted lady.

At the beginning of this book, I stated that my cross-cultural stories and the masterpiece projects on which I worked preceded the global financial meltdown. That statement has been true, exclusive of one glaring actuality: the effects of the global recession were delayed a year in their arrival to the Gulf countries, cushioned by a sense of financial immortality. New real estate development projects in the UAE totaling $137 billion were announced at Cityscape in Dubai in late 2008. The announcement ironically coincided with the detection of financial tremors felt elsewhere in the world. An abrupt reversal of construction activity began in 2009 with $960 billion—almost a *trillion*—worth of real estate developments in the UAE restructured, placed on hold, or canceled. These are staggering numbers for a dinky country! Dubai alone shelved one-half of its construction projects in 2009. Speculative investment money flooding the market focused on third-party developers, and they had lost their appetite.

Many friends and other Westerners had invested in the skyrocketing real estate market in the UAE prior to late 2008. They frantically bought and sold homes often before building was begun, let alone completed. Greed turned to tears when property values dropped by as much as 60 percent in 2009–2011. The widely shared 2012 forecast is a continuing downward spiral over the next two to three years. Unable to apply the brakes, developers continued to flood the already oversupplied market into 2011, further compounding the country's depressed property—not *energy*—sector. A residual supply of eleven thousand new homes and commercial space were unloaded in Abu Dhabi alone in the fourth quarter of 2011. Dubai and Abu Dhabi seem to be in a competition to create residential ghost towns. At the time of this writing, it is no surprise that the demand for new housing in Abu Dhabi and Dubai remains as stagnant as a lake covered in algae. The Rulers realized that their plans were too ambitious and that many of the projects didn't make as much economic sense as they had initially thought.

The waning demand for property has been devastating to my former employer, the largest real estate development company in the emirate of Abu Dhabi. Its stock price plunged 92 percent between early 2007 and late 2011. It became a penny stock. The government "rescued" the company in January 2011 with a $5.2 billion emergency support package that enabled it to continue with assorted construction projects. A second government bailout to reduce the company's indebtedness and deleverage its balance sheet was completed in December 2011. That complex $4.6 billion deal was structured around hard and soft prized-asset transfers and reimbursements. Mubadala, the government's investment branch, then held ownership of nearly 60 percent of the company, although its position is declared as "not-direct government ownership." Baffling. Mysteriously and conveniently, the value placed on the company's substantial land bank in Abu Dhabi appreciated to further aid in offsetting its indebtedness. The rules governing accounting practices are opaque. If recent history proves telling, the government will continue to provide creative rescue funding so that the company will not continue to be a coffee room topic of discussion at Moody's, Standard & Poor's, or Fitch. Moody's had already downgraded the company to negative and B3 in 2011. The drop from an AAA to a B3 rating in four years was a classic case of investing a phenomenal amount of money in snazzy infrastructure and in the commercial and residential real estate bubble without monitoring absorbency expectations.

The nearly $10 billion that the Abu Dhabi government has now invested in the development company is in addition to the $10 billion it extended to the emirate of Dubai in 2009 to assist in reducing its overwhelming debt. Only the Rulers of the two emirates will ever know what equity was exchanged in that rescue gift.

Consumer confidence in the UAE's property sector remains low for a number of unique reasons, aside from tight money. Basic elements of property ownership were placed on a back burner, or ignored, throughout most of the building frenzy in 2006–2009. Who would foot the bill to maintain the common grounds of a completed development? Garbage collection, janitorial services, landscape maintenance, lightbulb replacement, window washing, sand removal from walkways, repainting stripes in parking areas, and the servicing of air-conditioning units were a few of the many oversights. No level of facilities management had been factored into the cost of ownership. The buyer of a housing unit had no idea what a service fee was, let alone what one might include. The property developer didn't either. It was not until well after a sale was consummated, in most cases, that chaos reared its ugly head. A property owner had little clout to challenge unfulfilled promises. Cases arose in Dubai where residents moved into a unit in a "completed" high-rise building that was powered by generators because the municipal power company had not yet run power lines to it. Word spread quickly throughout the property sector that home ownership may be a can of worms. The government began to address the fallout literally after the fact.

Foreigners who had flocked to the UAE in 2006–2007 departed in 2009–2011 by the tens of thousands. A report surfaced stating that tens of thousands of expat work visas in Dubai alone were not renewed. In 2009, Dubai's population declined 8 percent. Many unemployed expats who fled the country abandoned their cars at Dubai's airport rather than risk jail time for defaulting on their auto loans. Keys were left in the ignitions in many of the estimated three thousand abandoned vehicles. The Brits who fled the UAE did not have to worry about creditors because most of the Emirati banks have no affiliation with British financial institutions. Those same Brits, however, will not be received with open arms should they decide to return. A crispy-warm desert jail that does not serve bangers and mash would be a disappointment.

In the brief four-year window of 2006 through 2009, Abu Dhabi and Dubai entered and exited one of the most unbridled and frenetic growth cycles seen in the twentieth and twenty-first centuries. The unprecedented vertical peak and valley could be duplicated only on an EKG. The remarkable achievements within the economic bubble may never be equaled by any country in the foreseeable future. They were years of pure, unadulterated opportunity. The expectations of Abu Dhabi's Rulers were, and still are, exceedingly high. The Rulers believed then, and still do today, that the unachievable *can* be achieved, albeit now at a reduced velocity.

Even though Abu Dhabi continues to harvest staggering liquidity and is ruled by a well-entrenched, nontyrannical Royal Family, it may not spend its energy-sourced revenue indiscriminately. Fiscal restraint and prudent governance are being exercised. When signs of economic vibrancy reappear, Abu Dhabi will be leaner, meaner, and well equipped to take advantage of the financial hiccup. Dubai, on the other hand, has a tarnished image and a mountain of debt to dig out from under. And yet, its enormous scale retains a global allure, and its economy has proven to be amazingly resilient. Dubai cannot be counted out by *any* stretch of the imagination. Abu Dhabi, however, has assumed the reins of progress in the UAE and will likely continue to lead the way. But prolonged visionary leadership, regulatory evolution, expat ingenuity, and investor confidence must interface to trigger a return to economic vitality in the property sector. Fortunately for Abu Dhabi, its vast reservoirs of crude oil and natural gas cushion an economic downturn and are an insurance policy underwritten by oil-thirsty countries that guarantees the country's progress.

Rome was not built overnight. Abu Dhabi came close, and so did Dubai. It is only 2012. Abu Dhabi can afford the luxury of patience.

Pleasure Boating?

My experience with recreational boating originated in the San Francisco Bay and its delta tributaries. There are many times more private powerboats and sailboats in this area than in the entire Arabian Gulf, which includes the UAE, Oman, Qatar, Bahrain, Saudi Arabia, Kuwait, and Iran. The sport is enjoyed by tens of thousands of outdoorsy people—men and women, young and old, single and married, wealthy and indebted college students—seeking relaxation, an outlet, a business rendezvous, a party, mental therapy, or a challenge. The Bay becomes a sea of sails on weekends. Races, regattas, fishing excursions, raft-ups, individual day outings, and vacation cruises all compete for attention. Waterfront restaurants, yacht clubs, and sheltered coves offer inviting destinations. Pleasure boating in the United States is a lifestyle—an established culture.

I admit I was caught up in the glow of a shooting star that the rest of the world knew as Dubai. My entire marina team was captivated. Opulence flourished. I believed I could provide the leadership to create a recreational boating lifestyle in Abu Dhabi. The master planners incorporated computer-generated, conceptual drawings and virtual-reality DVDs in their circus presentations to the company's senior management and Rulers. Their work was over the top and inspirational and was embraced with open arms. It was taken for granted that future property buyers would be loaded with cash. After all, it *is* Abu Dhabi. Thousands of the buyers would certainly purchase pleasure boats to adorn the floating pontoons in front of their expensive waterfront villas or to place in a new state-of-the-art marina. No problem. What was overlooked was that there is a *middle* class, however that is defined in the highest-income-per-capita city on the planet. The middle class historically comprises the bulk of buyers of most every commodity in the developed world. The wealthier may own Ikea and its inventory, but the middle class purchases the six-packs of potholders. The middle class has the investors who would escalate the occupancy rate in newly constructed marinas.

My assumption that a mature pleasure-boating culture was already entrenched in Abu Dhabi proved to be incorrect. I glossed over the reality that I was on a fast-track mission to introduce ownership of a recreational fiberglass boat to countrymen with a wooden dhow mentality. My responsibility was not a simple matter of being handed a baton and sprinting to the finish line. There was no baton. The realization was sobering. It was analogous to skipping high school en route to college and having to backtrack to fill in the academic blanks necessary to function intelligently. It would be a grueling path to navigate. But I was mentally prepared for the challenge.

The privileged lifestyle inherited by Abu Dhabians has evolved with extraordinary speed, but history reveals that change evolves over unhurried time. Caution accompanies change. To a formidable degree, the foundation blocks necessary to successfully cope with Abu Dhabi's changing times are only partially in place. The country's vigilance resulting from economic chaos is now providing time for visionaries to reevaluate, reformulate, and remove tinted glasses. Economic yield signs are providing the emirate's citizens the time to digest their relatively newfound wealth and determine how, where, and on what to spend their money. A pleasure boat may not rank high on their shopping lists today. There is justification.

Weather, class-based society, male-female cultural norms, cost of boat ownership, restricted boating waters, and strategic geographic locale all vie to handicap the development of recreational boating in the country. Not to be ignored, the surplus of housing, mostly unaffordable, creates economic uncertainty. To cite an overused American cliché: "Other than that, Mrs. Lincoln, how was the play?"

For half the year, the desert heat becomes uncomfortable for many people. The sun's intense rays and their reflection off a vessel's white deck and the sparkling turquoise water can be blinding. Air-conditioning assists in neutralizing the heat, but it provides cooled air only in an enclosed space on a vessel and is insufficient to cool an exterior deck area, where much of the enjoyment from being on the water is derived.

Very few Emiratis who own, or hope to own, a pleasure boat theoretically exceeding twelve meters (forty feet) will personally insert a key in its ignition. In the class-based society, protocol calls for a vessel to be operated, provisioned, fueled, and maintained by others. Chances are slim to none that a Muslim lady will participate in a pleasure-boat outing without a chaperone or her immediate family because of the male-female cultural norms. Yacht manufacturers in the Middle East have only recently begun to incorporate separate salons, or gathering areas, below deck to accommodate men separately from women. Their sensitivity to Islamic principles is a gigantic step in the right direction.

Practically speaking, today's pleasure boats are not cheap, at least from my perspective. Prices for a new twelve-meter luxury boat may begin in the neighborhood of four hundred to six hundred thousand dollars, and the price tag increases exponentially with length. A non-Emirati resident is essentially eliminated from the marketplace because of cost.

Restricted navigable waters, privately owned islands in Abu Dhabi's archipelago of sandbars, and national security take precedence over a desire to randomly pleasure cruise. The heavily patrolled areas can easily raise a pleasure boater's anxiety level, as I and many other friends and colleagues experienced. A fear of the escalating Somalian piracy that had begun to encroach on formerly peaceful cruising waters in the Arabian Sea is another concern.

A marina with low occupancy spells bankruptcy in the Western world. It is a business like any other commercial undertaking. Whether it is privately or government-owned, it cannot, or should not, remain operable if it does not generate enough revenue to at least break even. This rule simply, and without surprise, does not apply in Abu Dhabi. All waterfront property, which includes marinas, is owned or heavily invested in, as designed by the government, by Abu

Dhabi nationals, many of whom possess a genetic tie to the Ruling Family. Also by lawful understanding, nationals retain ownership or sponsorship of at least 51 percent of each and every business on Abu Dhabi soil (at the time of my residency). Money may therefore be made available, directly or indirectly, from an overflowing government cash register to satisfy a financial shortcoming. There are no concrete rules. The emirate of Abu Dhabi is small enough that most all Emirati businessmen of financial consequence are familiar with one another's investments. The importance of saving face is paramount. An unprofitable profit-and-loss statement may occupy second position behind a dazzling visible attraction for the eyes of the world. The two recently completed, high-tech marinas from my original fifteen-marina and boat service center portfolio *are* dazzling, the best of the best. Unfortunately, the tanked economy has contributed to an unfeasibly high vacancy rate. The marinas will, however, survive. In Abu Dhabi, bankruptcy as it is known in the Western world simply does not occur.

Am I pleased with our accomplishments? Absolutely. They are profound steps in the big picture of furthering the evolution of a boating lifestyle in an emerged country. My marina team invested an immense amount of their combined talent and energy in the three-year endeavor to achieve my initial goal. We brought together multiple government agencies to recognize and refine waterway laws and guidelines. Entry and exit visa requirements for boaters were streamlined. The Sheikhs' expectations were met in building a masterpiece marina central to the Formula One racetrack. Yas Marina and its yacht club have been added to the esteemed list of premier global yachting destinations. The marina has been featured in all of the glossy international yachting magazines and viewed on TV by hundreds of millions of people, and its website is stunning. The inaugural Abu Dhabi International Yacht Show in 2008 was timed to highlight the construction of Yas Marina. Several of the world's largest megayachts and yacht brokerages attended the exclusive event. The Rulers capped the finale with a black-tie gala dinner at the Emirates Palace while the yachts paraded off its beach, basked in a spectacular laser light show.

Will another three or five years of dedicated work significantly boost the growth of a user-friendly location for recreational boating? I wish for a magic wand. In 2007, I told the company's CEO that I believed Abu Dhabi to be "a mecca of yacht-purchasing power." Purchasing power it has. Geographical location it has not. Regional peace is the white knight awaiting arrival.

Part Eleven

---◆◆◆---

Entrepreneurial Nomads

Like most Western expatriates, Pamela and I elected to expand our occupational, intellectual, creative, and cultural spheres and witness values through the eyes of others. We made the choice to temporarily exchange a comfortable life in California with family members, friends, and an existence where likes are more likely to hang with likes in order to pursue these goals. Many Western expats are accused of being entrepreneurial nomads at heart. We were no exception.

Our relocation to Abu Dhabi without family or friends present to share experiences and emotions was a momentous adjustment. Social energies were redirected. Quality friendships were a challenge to establish because of cultural diversity. Overcoming behavioral idiosyncrasies and convictions required effort. Although most expats were multilingual, the search for the appropriate word or phrase was nonetheless a continuous struggle. Most Westerners who speak a second language generally do not speak Arabic, Farsi, or one of the many Asian languages or dialects. Our ability to laugh at ourselves or together with unabashed openness proved to be refreshing.

New acquaintances faced identical challenges. They were equally as interested in our opinions, our food, and a good party. Over time, we developed bonds with Canadians, Aussies, Kiwis, South Africans, Lebanese, Jordanians, Iraqis, Iranians, Russians, Eastern and Western Europeans, and Emiratis. I cheered with the French,

Brits, New Zealanders, Australians, and South Africans whilst (ha, got it!) watching rugby matches. My doctor was from Turkey, my dentist from Iceland. Pamela spent mornings at desert horse farms riding with British and South African equestrian friends. We shared dinners, laughed, argued, and partied into the wee hours with newfound expat and Emirati friends. Our strong camaraderie continues today, two years following our relocation back to California. Invitations to stay or visit with those friends in their homelands have been exchanged, accepted, and honored. Expats' efforts to establish quality friendships provide a rich bonus.

The peace-loving people from the many countries with whom I interacted daily shared a common trait that formed a link between us: acceptance of others. I developed friendships with more Iranian, Iraqi, Syrian, Egyptian, and Pakistani expats than I have friends in California. They were born, raised, and continue to have citizenship in countries declared suspect today by the United States—and that goes both ways. Those proclaiming the suspicion, distrust, animosity—call it what they will—are generally the roosters from each henhouse. Agreeably, leaders—be they elected, appointed, inherited, or imposed—serve, in *most* cases, an indispensable function in orchestrating a sound economic, political, social, military, and religious structure. That being what it is, my collection of international friends and colleagues and their families—call us the hens—felt secure lounging around a pool together and drinking lemonade, watching kids play, and laughing until our bellies hurt. That, for me, is a beautiful, rich, emotional, and unforgettable part of cross-cultural assimilation.

We worked hard and played hard in and around this tiny spot on the globe. New experiences entered our paths virtually every day and created a level of sustained awareness. Most were uplifting and eye-opening, while others were trying—a product of our Western interpretation. But the collection was contagious. We wanted more, like handful after handful of popcorn or Doritos. The rewards derived proved to be proportionate to our level of open-mindedness and ability to focus on the lighter side of life.

I laugh now reflecting on the number of times we got lost and the number of sandals we wore out. Acclimation to the heat was not difficult in that Pamela and I prefer warm to chilly weather. We sat out a blinding sandstorm in our car and also viewed the heaven of stars on crystal clear nights from desert dunes. We attended horse races, traditional desert parties, and Bollywood film festivals and rode camels. We dune bashed, snowboarded sand dunes, smoked shishas, traveled to ten other countries, and learned words in multiple languages. We learned the meaning of Ramadan and shared Eid with Muslim friends. We were guests at Royals' palaces, horse stables, and a falcon-breeding facility. We toured the Grand Mosque and ascended the Burj Al Arab and Burj Al Khalifa in Dubai. We saw Bon Jovi, Andrea Bocelli, Beyoncé, George Michael, Aerosmith, Alicia Keys, and Yo-Yo Ma in concert and danced Arabian-style at private parties. We ate with our fingers in zero-star ethnic dives and in five-star restaurants catered by Michelin chefs. We skin-dived in the warm, clear waters of Musandam in Oman near the Straits of Hormuz, where goats are smuggled in hundreds of fast boats from Iran to waiting offshore Omani dhows. We plied the waterways in dhows and abras and attended yacht shows in Monaco, Saint-Tropez, Cannes, and Nice and were guests on several of the world's largest private luxury yachts. And we viewed deafening Formula One races in Monaco and, of course, Abu Dhabi. Most importantly, Pamela and I shared these extraordinary unplanned experiences as best friends—the pinnacle of a marriage vow.

We departed the country as quickly as we had entered. Bing, bang, boom. The Rulers decreed that it was time to apply the brakes, and I was included in the massive expat redundancies in 2009, the beginning of the postponed economic meltdown in Abu Dhabi. The work visa of a resident expat is canceled when he is made redundant, and without a work visa, the residency visa is canceled. Without a residency visa, a continued stay in the UAE requires a renewable sixty-day visitor's visa along with medical insurance coverage, a significant expense. Migrant workers are required to leave the country within forty-eight hours following cancellation of their work permits. The country's expat unemployment rate is *theoretically* 0 percent. The built-in safety net minimizes the risk of social unrest due to unemployment. There is no need for unemployment insurance. Then again, there are no tax withholdings.

My non-American friends had no qualms about teasing me regarding their preferred income tax structure. An expat from a country *other* than the United States is not subject to taxation on foreign-earned income. If he or she earns a hundred thousand dollars per year, he or she pockets a hundred thousand dollars. The United States is the only developed country that taxes foreign-earned income. Only after residency is established in a foreign country (based on a government formula) does a US expat qualify for an income tax exclusion on just shy of the first ninety thousand earned. (The exclusion is adjusted annually for inflation, if any.) In other words, if a US expat earns a hundred thousand dollars per year, he or she is subject to income tax on ten thousand, with ninety thousand dollars excluded from taxation. Double that for a married working couple.

I am pained to see the continuance of redundancies into 2012 for thousands of world-class, talented expatriates in Abu Dhabi's nonpetroleum sectors. Many of the former positions are being filled by nationals, many of whom do not possess the educational background, credentials, and experience that have elevated the country to emerged-world status in record time. The emirate's growth may lay fallow, not because of a lack of money but because of the loss of many critical thinkers to blaze a path. Salvation will hopefully come from the government's astute shift to favoring joint-venture business relationships with international powerhouse companies that will establish a physical presence on Abu Dhabi sand and educate and integrate nationals into the workforce. The nonpetroleum sector will continue to thrive, generating over 50 percent of Abu Dhabi's GDP, contrary to the widely held belief that revenue from oil exports accounts for the lion's share.

Departing Western expats, surprisingly, did not leave behind most of the "attached" items that they had purchased for their villas. The kitchen appliances, wall and ceiling light fixtures, and eight-foot-high window coverings throughout our 465-square-meter villa and a landscaped yard were a 50,000 dirham ($13,700) out-of-pocket investment. That was light compared to what was spent by most of the other expats, particularly those with children. Our compound was owned by a member of the Royal Family who could easily afford to purchase a team in the National Football League. He was making out like a bandit by having his lessees pay to landscape his compound, which consisted of hundreds of villas. I noticed that departing expats advertised their appliances, unwanted furniture, draperies, vehicles, and plants on bulletin boards in the Spinneys grocery stores. Some expats even cut and rolled-up their lawns, or sod, to sell upon termination of their lease. Sure enough, the household items and plants on the long, itemized list that was tacked to the bulletin board, including our two vehicles, all sold within one week. The buyer of the six mature bougainvillea shrubs that bordered our backyard patio brought a shovel and clay pots to facilitate removal. If it was possible to sell sand, I could have retired. Including the cars, we were pleased to recoup 50–60 percent of our original investment. I stuck by my principle to not further pad a wealthy landlord's investment. I rationalized my actions as being fiscally responsible, not malicious, in a system that allowed such behavior.

The announcement of our impending departure to two of the fine gentlemen who had provided impeccable domestic services for us was heart-wrenching. Ajit, a tall Indian from Kerala, washed our two vehicles (including those of guests, if requested) and the villa's exterior walkway for nearly three years. Sanjeev, a handsome Sri Lankan, performed any domestic task that was asked of him, from laying patio pavers to moving furniture to washing the company boat. They took immense pride in their work, and we compensated them with an above-average amount of dirham. Both of them asked if we would take them back to the States. To them, our sponsorship represented a new life in the land of the free and a chance to continue working for people who demonstrated appreciation for their efforts. From a practical standpoint, the sand dust that haunts everyday life in the UAE does not exist in California. We do not have young children who might benefit from a nanny, and we enjoy doing our own grocery shopping. Our residence does not have living quarters for a housekeeper, and our expense budget does not include a larger household. The disappointment reflected in the eyes of Ajit and Sanjeev ripped a hole in our hearts when we explained that we could not oblige their request. The rebellion against servitude imposed on the labor class by most all Western expats and nationals, which I had felt beginning on day one in the UAE, surfaced and left a terrible taste in my mouth. I felt helpless. There was not a damn thing I could do about it. I was a guest in a country with a blatant de facto caste system that, for the present, worked for it.

The years of 2006, 2007, 2008, and 2009 were four of the more exciting boom years in the development of a piece of real estate—on sand, no less. They were gold-rush years. Abu Dhabi's landscape changed remarkably. From my construction background, it was unimaginable entertainment. *Iconic, off-the-chart, largest, tallest, fastest, opulent,* and *dazzling* are some of the words used to describe the masterpiece that began on a blank canvas a decade ago. The manpower, raw materials, and heavy machinery required to complete the projects in this tiny country strained the global markets. *Abu Dhabi* became a household word in international circles. Little did I envision that I would be thrown headfirst into an integral role in placing Abu Dhabi on the map as a premier global yachting destination. My footprint remains. Nor did I anticipate being overwhelmed by the diversity of experiences and, in many ways, a privileged lifestyle. Luck played its role in being in the right place at the right time. Guts and a gamble made it happen.

What would I have done differently in my formative years as a young adult to prepare for integration on an international level? I would have viewed life from a global perspective, a quest requiring scholarly curiosity; become proficient in another language, preferably two; and traveled internationally as often as the pocketbook would allow. The phenomenon of globalization had not taken hold until the late 1990s. I was a certificated adult before then. The world, at that time, was becoming more accessible, and global talent was becoming a sought-after commodity. *Outsourcing* and *offshoring* became buzzwords for economic growth and competition. College enrollment in the fields of computer science and engineering—two fields that I did not pursue—was escalating. With the rare exception, an advanced university degree guaranteed greater opportunities, especially overseas. Knowledge was king. Drive and self-confidence accompany knowledge and are key to integration in an unfamiliar world.

Our odyssey to superlatives was a 3-D, wide-screen journey. I likened the e-ticket ride to the world's fastest roller coaster, Formula

Rossa, completed in late 2010 in Ferrari World on Yas Island. Fast is accelerating from 0 to 100 kilometers per hour (0 to 60 miles per hour) in 2.8 seconds, hitting 240 kilometers per hour (149 miles per hour) and experiencing g-forces to 4.8.

Would we do it all over again? In a heartbeat. I would first acknowledge to Mr. Webster and Mr. Oxford that I comprehend their definitions of *open-minded* and *patience* in two languages— American and Brit, *insha'Allah.*

References

"Abu Dhabi Company for Onshore Oil Operations: Products & Services." *Abu Dhabi National Oil Company.* June 2011. http://www.adnoc.ae

Abu Dhabi Grand Prix: Etihad Racing. Etihad Airways. December 2011. http://www.etihadracing.com/EtihadRacing/AUH

"Abu Dhabi—Profile of Geographical Entity Including Name Variants." *World Gazetteer.* April 8, 2008. http://www.worldgazetteer.com

"Abu Dhabi Sovereign Wealth Fund Starts to Open Up." *The Star-Business.* March 15, 2010. http://www.adia.ae

Al-Fahim, Mohammed. *From Rags to Riches: A Story of Abu Dhabi.* London Center of Arab Studies. 1995: 19, 75, 147.

Al-Mulhim, Abdulateef. "Strait of Hormuz and Iranian threats." *Arab News.* January 7, 2012. http://www.arabnews.com

Al Shami, Abdallah. "A Caravan through Time." *Shawati: Imprints of Abu Dhabi*. March 2009. Under the Patronage of HE Sheikh Sultan Bin Tahnoon Al Nahyan. 51–59.

Arun, MG. "Abu Dhabi Sovereign Fund Mulls India Entry." *The Financial Express*. March 11, 2011.
http://www.financialexpress.com/news/abu-dhabis-sovereign-fund

Burton, Steve. "Abu Dhabi Marina Development: Strategy and Recommendations." March 2009.

"Camels Strut Their Stuff at Abu Dhabi Pageant." *Islam Forum*. December 18, 2010.
http://www.topix.com/forum/religion/islam/T46E88PPU22UQ1RLT

"Country Analysis Briefs." *Oil & Gas Journal*. January 2011. Energy Information Administration. United Arab Emirates Energy Data, Statistics and Analysis. 1–9.
http://www.eia.gov/countries/cab.cfm?fips=TC

"Formula 1 Global TV Audience Expands." *Paddock Talk*. January 2009.
http://www.paddocktalk.com/news/html/story-100719.html.

Goodbody, James. "Gearing for Greatness." *Shawati, Imprints of Abu Dhabi, HE Mohamed Khalaf Al Mazrouei*. January 2009. Under the Patronage of HE Sheikh Sultan Bin Tahnoon Al Nahyan. Issue 8. 142–49.

"Gulf Real Estate Development Breaks through $1 Trillion." October 2007. http://www.albawaba.com. http://www.projectsandleads.com (charts). http://www.ameinfo.com

John, Isaac. "Aldar to Sell Assets to Abu Dhabi Government in Dh16.8b Deal." *Khaleej Times.* October 29, 2011.

"List of UAE Naturalization and Residency Departments." *UAE Immigration.* November 10, 2009. http://www.dubaifaqs.com/immigration-uae.php

Maddux, W. W., and A. D. Galinsky. "Cultural borders and mental barriers: The relationship between living abroad and creativity." *Journal of Personality and Social Psychology,* 96(5). May 2009. pp. 1047–61. Reprinted with permission from American Psychological Association.

"Maintenance and Management Can Generate Strong Revenues for the Gulf's Maritime Industry." *Luxury Yacht Charter & Superyacht News.* March 30, 2011. Charter World. http://www.charterworld.com

Nellen, Alain. "Desalinization: A viable answer to deal with the water crises?" *Future Directions International.* July 2011.

OPEC Annual Statistical Bulletin. 2010–2011 Edition. http://www.opec.org_web/static_files_project/media/downloads/publications/ASB2010_2011.pdf

"The People of Yas Island." *Yas Island: Race to the Finish.* DVV Media Middle East FZ LLC. 2009:40.

Plan Abu Dhabi 2030: Urban Structure Framework Plan. Urban Planning Council. 2009. http://www.upc.gov.ae/abu-dhabi-2030

"Projects Worth Dh.500 bn Announced at Cityscape Dubai 2008."
Estates Dubai, Dubai Real Estate News—UAE Property. October 10,
2008.
http://www.estatesdubai/2008/10/projects-worth-dh500bn-announce

Rosenberg, David. "UAE Population Up by 65% in Four Years." *The
Media Line.* UAE National Statistics Bureau. April 3, 2011: 22, 35.
http://www.arabnews.com

"Sovereign Wealth Fund Rankings. Largest SWFs by Assets Under
Management." *Institute Fund Summit 2012.* Sovereign Wealth Fund
Institute. http://www.swfinstitute.org/fund-rankings/

Stabile, Matt. "How Many Americans Own a Passport?" *The
Expeditioner.* January 6, 2011.
http://www.theexhibitioner.com/tag/number-of-americans-passport

Statistical Yearbook: Abu Dhabi 2010. Statistics Centre (SCAD). Abu
Dhabi (2010): 17, 57, 62, 102. http://www.scad.ae

"UAE Economic Brief and Outlook." *KAMCO Research.* April 2011.
KIPCO Asset Management Company KSC. 2–26.
http://www.kamconline.com

"UAE Population." *CIA World Factbook.* January 2012.
http://www.cia.gov/library/publications/the-world-factbook/geos/
ae.html

"UAE World's Top Water Consumer." *Emirates 24/7.* September
20, 2011.
http://www.emirates247.com/business/economy-finance/uae-world

Verma, Sonia. "Driven Down by Debt, Dubai Expats ..." *The Times* and *The Sunday Times*. February 5, 2009.
http://www.arabbusiness.com

Walsh, John. "UAE: Customs and Culture." *Culture Smart*. 2011. pp. 10, 89, 123, 150, 152.
http://www.culturesmartguides.com

About the Author

Steve Burton, a marina development consultant, cultural adviser, and author, received his bachelor of arts at the University of California at Davis and master of arts at San Francisco State University. He spent twenty years in the real estate development and  construction industries, followed by eight years in the maritime industry—all in Northern California. Combining his background experiences, he relocated to Abu Dhabi in the United Arab Emirates in 2007. His work in the Middle East earned him international acclaim and recognition as one of today's premier marina specialists. He and his wife live in the San Francisco Bay Area.

Made in the USA
Lexington, KY
16 April 2013